D1420588

A STUDY OF PUBLIC POLICY INFLUENCES UPON THE
DEVELOPMENT OF CHINA'S RURAL ENTERPRISES 1978-1992

A Study of Public Policy Influences upon the Development of China's Rural Enterprises 1978-1992

WANG ZHONGHUI

Avebury

Aldershot • Brookfield USA • Hong Kong • Singapore • Sydney

Published by
Avebury
Ashgate Publishing Limited
Gower House
Croft Road
Aldershot
Hants GU11 3HR
England

Ashgate Publishing Company
Old Post Road
Brookfield
Vermont 05036
USA

British Library Cataloguing in Publication Data
Wang, Zhonghui
　　A study of public policy influences upon the development of
　　China's rural enterprises, 1978-1992
　　1.Rural industries - China - Government policy 2.China -
　　Economic policy - 1976 -
　　I.Title
　　322.3'0951

Library of Congress Catalog Card Number: 96-79121

ISBN 1 85972 543 0

Printed and bound by Athenaeum Press, Ltd.,
Gateshead, Tyne & Wear.

Contents

Acknowledgements

I would like to express my appreciation for comments and suggestions from Dr.S. Breslin and Professor. T. Gray in the Department of Politics, University of Newcastle upon Tyne, and Dr. I Weir in the Department of Economics, University of Newcastle upon Tyne over several years. In particular, Chapter Three in this book has benefited from Dr. S. Breslin's research on Centre-Province relations in China.

I also want to express my thanks for the use of materials provided by the Sinological Institute, University of Leiden, and for the comments of the part of my study by Professor T. Saich and Dr. E. B. Vermeer at Leiden University, The Netherlands, Dr. F. Christiansen, University of Leeds, England. This book has also benefited from stylistic improvements from Mrs. Anne Gray and Ms. Rachel Walmsley.

Some information of this study has already appeared in the following articles: 'Private Enterprise in China: An Overview', *The Journal of Communist Studies* (now called *The Journal of Communist Studies and Transition Politics*), Vol.6, No.3, 1990, pp.83-98, 'China's Policies Towards Collective Rural Enterprises', *Small Enterprise Development*, Vol.4, No.1, 1993, pp.16-26, and 'Township Public Finance and Its Impact on the Financial Burden of Rural Enterprises and Peasants in Mainland China', *Issues and Studies*, Vol.31, No.8, 1995, pp.103-121. I wish to express my thanks to these journals for allowing me to reproduce parts of my articles in this book.

Abbreviations

ADR	*Asian Development Review*
AJCA	*The Australian Journal of Chinese Affairs* (now called *The China Journal*)
AS	*Asian Survey*
BR	*Beijing Review*
BYT	*Banyue Tan* (Semi-Monthly Talks)
CCP	Chinese Communist Party
CD	*China Daily*
CES	*Chinese Economic Studies*
CI	*China Information*
CJKX	*Caijing Kexue* (Science of Finance and Economics)
CQ	*The China Quarterly*
CR	*China Reconstructs*
CT	*China Today*
DGB	*Dagong Bao* (Dagong Daily)
FBIS	*Foreign Broadcast Information Service*
FEER	*Far Eastern Economic Review*
GJMYWT	*Guoji Maoyi Wenti* (Problems of International Trade)
GNP	Gross National Product
GMRB	*Guangming Ribao* (Guangming Daily)
GSXZGL	*Gongshang Xingzheng Guanli* (Industry and Business Administration)
ICM	*Inside China Mainland*

IS	*Issues & Studies*
JCS	*The Journal of Communist Studies* (now called *The Journal of Communist Studies and Transition Politics*)
JFRB	*Jiefang Ribao* (Liberation Daily)
JJCK	*Jingji Cankao* (Economic References)
JJGZTX	*Jingji Gongzuo Tongxun* (Economic Work Bulletin)
JJYJCKZL	*Jingji Yangjiu Cankao Ziliao* (Reference Material for Economic Studies)
JJWT	*Jingji Wenti* (Economic Problems)
JJZB	*Jingji Zhoubao* (Economy Weekly)
JJRB	*Jingji Ribao* (Economic Daily)
JJYFL	*Jingji Yu Falu* (Economy and Law)
JJYJ	*Jingji Yanjiu* (Economic Research)
JPRS	*Joint Publications Research Services*
JRSB	*Jinrong Shibao* (Financial Times)
LW	*Liaowang* (Outlook Weekly)
NCCWKJ	*Nongcun Caiwu Kuaiji* (Rural Financial Accounting)
NCJR	*Nongcun Jinrong* (Rural Finance)
NMRB	*Nongmin Ribao* (Peasant Daily)
NPC	National People's Congress
NYJJ	*Nongye Jingji* (Agricultural Economy)
NYJJWT	*Nongye Jingji Wenti* (Problems of Agricultural Economy)
NYKJYJ	*Nongye Kuaiji Yanjiu* (Agricultural Accounting Research)
PC	*Problems of Communism*
PRC	People's Republic of China
QS	*Qiushi* (Seeking Truth)
RMB	Renminbi
RMRB	*Renmin Ribao* (People's Daily)
SCRB	*Sichuan Ribao* (Sichuan Daily)
SED	*Small Enterprise Development*
SHKXDT	*Shehui Kexue Dongtai* (Social Science Trends)
SHKXZX	*Shehui Kexue Zhanxian* (Social Science Front)
SJJJDB	*Shijie Jingji Daobao* (International Economic Herald)
SSIC	*Social Sciences in China*
SWB/FE	*Summary of World Broadcasts/Far East/Daily Report*
SWB/FE/W	*Summary of World Broadcasts/Far East/Weekly Economic Report*
TE	*The Economist*
XHYB	*Xinhua Yuebao* (New China Monthly)

XXYYJ	*Xuexi Yu Yanjiu* (Study and Research)
KJGLYJ	*Keji Guanli Yanjiu* (Studies on Scientific Management)
WGYZL	*Wengao Yu Zilio* (Manuscripts and Materials)
ZGJJWT	*Zhongguo Jingji Wenti* (Chinese Economic Problems)
ZGNCJJ	*Zhongguo Nongcun Jingji* (Chinese Rural Economy)
ZGSW	*Zhongguo Shuiwu* (China's Taxes)
ZGXZQYB	*Zhongguo Xiangzhen Qiye Bao* (Chinese Township and Town Enterprise Daily)

1 Introduction

The significance of the study

For many third world nations, the axiom that 'big is best' seems to have been at the heart of economic development strategies. The establishment of large industrial complexes has been seen as the key to laying the foundations for further economic development and the creation of a vibrant domestic economy. However, the evidence of recent years is that the expected economic growth and increased employment that large scale industrialization was supposed to generate have been slow in appearing. As a result, many development economists have increasingly turned their attention to the potential impact of emphasizing the development of small scale enterprises.

This shift in emphasis has been reflected by the actions of many national governments. Some developing countries have intensified their measures to support and protect such enterprises. In contrast to the traditional large scale complexes, small scale enterprises are thought to have made significant contributions to both employment generation and the diffusion of skills and technology. These developments have been reflected by the growth in academic literature analyzing promotional policies adopted in developing countries for the development of small and medium scale industries.

Although large-scale state owned complexes played an important role in the Chinese economy from 1978 to 1992, rural enterprises had developed rapidly, and had become a major prop of the rural economy and an important part of the national economy. The following data clearly indicate rural enterprises' important role in China's national economy. In 1989, there were more than 18 million rural enterprises nationwide. They turned out 840.3 billion yuan in output value, an amount equal to the nation's entire 1979 gross product (Han Baocheng, 1990, p.13). In 1993, their output value reached 2,902 billion yuan (*CD*, 6 June 1994, p.4).

The development of rural enterprises had changed the old economic structure that was largely dependent on farmland and became a means by which the total output value of rural enterprises, as a proportion of that for rural society, increased from 31.4 percent in 1978 to 58 percent in 1989 and 71 per cent in 1993. From 1979 to 1989, rural enterprises ploughed more than 80 billion yuan from their profits back into rural undertakings (Han Baocheng, 1990, p.13, and *CD*, 6 June 1994, p.4). Without the contribution from rural enterprises, the financial situation for education, health care and welfare facilities in many rural areas would have been worse since local governments had faced fiscal restraints.

Rural enterprises had also become an outlet for the rural surplus labour force. In 1989, some 93.67 million people worked in rural enterprises, accounting for 23 per cent of the total rural labour force, or 62 per cent of the increased labour force from 1978 to 1989 (Han Baocheng, 1990, p.13).

Between 1979 and 1989, rural enterprises' direct subsidy of agricultural production was about one-third of the state investment in forestry, water conservancy and meteorology during the same period, thus considerably promoting agricultural production (Han Baocheng, 1990, p.14). In these 11 years, farmers across the country gained one-fourth of their net income from rural enterprises, and from 1986 to 1990, the proportion rose to 50 per cent (Han Baocheng, 1990, p.14). In 1993, their export reached 235 billion yuan ($27 billion), about 45 per cent of the country's total (*CD*, 6 June 1994, p.4).

The data such as the above show that developing rural enterprises had been a distinguishing characteristic of the rural development strategies in China. The development of rural enterprises had contributed immensely to the phenomenal growth of the rural economy and improved living standards in China's rural areas. The development of rural enterprises had also helped to boost agricultural production itself, while changing the traditional rural economic structure from one dominated by farming to a far more diversified economy. Furthermore, rural enterprises had played a very important role in providing rural employment, increasing financial revenue and earning foreign exchange.

Chinese government policy makers were also well aware of the importance of rural enterprises. For example, a 1984 joint State Council and Central Committee communique (The Minister of Agriculture, Animal Husbandry and Fishery and the Ministry's Leading Party Group (1984), *SWB/FE*, 26 March)

2

listed an impressive array of the beneficial consequences of allowing rural enterprises to flourish. The communique indicated that village and town enterprises were recognized as an important component of a diversified economy, an important pillar of agricultural production, an important way for the masses of peasants to achieve common prosperity, and an important source of state revenue. The development of village and town enterprises was further described as an important force in the national economy.

Given this laudative 'mid-term report', it is not surprising that some western observers had subscribed to the view that rural enterprises had well been on the way to changing the entire nature of Chinese society. For example, a report in *TE* suggested that: 'China's economy has produced a nice twist on Mao Zedong's theory of revolutionary war. The private enterprises of the countryside are surrounding, and threaten eventually to swamp the state-owned industries of the cities' (*TE*, 1 June 1991).

The year 1978 marks a watershed in the study of the importance of rural enterprises for the Chinese economy. Before this date, the dominance of 'leftist' ideology and, equally as important, the disbanding of economic research institutes meant that no research on rural enterprises was undertaken within China. Outside China, some western scholars, however, did undertake research on China's rural enterprises. The main focus of those works was rural industry, the main part of rural enterprises in China before 1978. The most important contributions to this field of study were *Rural Industrialization in China* by Jon Sigurdson (1977), and *Rural Small Scale Industry In The People's Republic of China* by the American Rural Small Scale Industry Delegation (1977). Jon Sigurdson focused his analysis on county run enterprises. He examined rural industrialization within counties, giving the rationale for the various programmes, an analysis of two model counties, and some estimate of how well the programmes worked. The crucial flaw in the American Rural Small-Scale Industry Delegation's work was that they interpreted what they were told, and failed to question the validity of the raw data they were given to work with.

In addition to these two books, two important articles are worthy of comment, namely 'Small Industry and the Chinese Model of Development' (Riskin, 1971, pp.245-273), and 'China's Rural Industries: 'Self-reliant Systems or Independent Kingdoms' both by Carl Riskin (1978, pp.77-98). The first article, published in 1971, examined the evolution and implementation of China's policy towards small and medium industry. In this article, the first four sections were concerned with the period of the First Five-Year Plan (1953-57), while the latter four dealt with the dramatic activities of the Great Leap Forward (1958-60) and the attempts to rationalize the small industry program in the 1960s.

Riskin's second article published in 1978 mainly dealt with the roots of these events in the development of China's rural industries from the 1960s. It evaluated the impact of the Cultural Revolution on rural industrialization, and sought to place the polemics over the socio-political implications of this form of development into the context of changing objective conditions. It is necessary to mention that the scope of all these works included county level state enterprises. Although this was a valid approach at the time, the definition of rural enterprises used in this study does not include county run enterprises. As a result, these earlier works have only a limited application to this study.

From 1978 to 1992, there had been an explosion of articles on rural enterprises within China. Some Chinese scholars had undertaken research on the position and characteristics of rural enterprises, and indeed disclosed much useful statistical information. However, inevitably many articles were deficient in that it lacked political analysis of the development of rural enterprises because of domestic political obstacles.

What is surprising is that although Chinese rural enterprises had developed dramatically from 1978 to 1992, few articles and books had been published in western countries in 1980s. In the early 1980s, the only articles of note were the following: 'Rural Enterprise in China, 1977-79' by Jack Gray (1982, pp.211-233), 'Commune and Brigade Run Enterprises in Rural China: an Overview' by Keith Griffin and Kimberley Griffin (1984, pp.210-222); and 'Commune- and Brigade-Run Industries in Rural China: Some Recent Observations' by J.L.Enos (1984, pp.223-252). Griffin and Griffin and Enos indicated a few of the characteristics, sizes of the commune and brigade enterprise sector, and briefly discussed some of the recent changes in policy affecting this sector. Gray described the growth, the regime and some changes of purpose in relation to rural enterprises, and discussed changes in the control of rural enterprises between 1977 and 1979.

Although these authors undoubtedly made some contribution to the literature on rural enterprises in China, their publications suffered from the following limitations. None paid any attention to the private sector of rural enterprises. It could be possible that their primary stumbling block might be lack of detailed information because the most debate and information concerning these sectors was not published in the Chinese press until the late 1980s.

In the late 1980s, more noteworthy articles were published. Two articles are especially worthy of comment: 'The Development of Town and Township Enterprises in Mainland China Since 1979' by Chen Tesheng (1986) and 'Policy, Practice and The Private Sector in China' by Susan Young (1989). The first article briefly discussed the theoretical basis for promoting town and

4

township enterprises, the evolution and characteristics of these enterprises, the reasons and measures for their development, as well as their advantages and disadvantages. The second article examined the growth of the private sector in China from 1978 to 1992, including the original goals of its promotion and development, and the impact of this growth on Chinese assessments of the role of private business in the Chinese economy. Without doubt, their articles have represented valuable research into rural enterprises and the private sector. However, the implications of other policy changes, such as rural employment and regional development policies, were not discussed. Policy analysis has also been inadequate.

The most important book on this subject is *China's Rural Industry: Structure, Development, and Reform* (Byrd and Ling, 1990). This six-part, nineteen-chapter volume is the result of a joint project by the World Bank and the Economics Institute of the Chinese Academy of Social Sciences. In 1986 and 1987, the joint World Bank and the Chinese Academy of Social Sciences research team conducted surveys and extensive interviews on China's township, village, and private enterprise sector. It is the first comprehensive study of China's township, village, and private enterprise sector based on systematic empirical evidence. The survey data collected as part of the project is comprehensive. The topics covered in the book, such as ownership, labour, efficiency, the role of governments, and comparative perspectives, are both theoretically and practically important. However, this research is not without its limitations. First, the research has been overtaken by the pace of change within China. As this research was completed before 1987, important changes that occurred after 1986 were not included. Secondly, there is the limitation of the analysis of public policy.

Therefore, as far as the literature reviewed above is concerned, research has tended to neglect the study of the impact of public policy on the development of rural enterprises. However, public policy has been extremely important in China since it has determined not only the extent to which rural enterprises have been developed, but also whether rural enterprises should be allowed to be developed at all! Therefore, an analysis of changes of public policy since 1978 must be a crucial component of any analysis of the development of rural enterprises.

In this study, I shall focus on policy changes towards the development of rural enterprises from 1978 to 1992. The policies towards the development of rural enterprises, especially private enterprises, had fiercely been debated during this period. Such debate had not been cooled down until Deng Xiaoping paid a visit to south China in early 1992, and called for bolder reforms.

The definition of rural enterprises

One of the problems entailed in studying rural enterprises in China is that of defining what constitutes 'rural enterprises'. There has been no united definition of rural enterprises, a problem exacerbated by the economic changes enacted after 1978. Before this date, the definition of rural enterprises was much broader than that used in the era of reform.

Carl Riskin gave the following definition: 'rural industries refer to those industries run by the rural communes and their production brigades and state industries at sub-provincial level, chiefly those operated by the hsien (county)' (Riskin, 1978, p.77). Jon Sigurdson's definition of 'rural industries' was similar to Carl Riskin's. Rural industry was, in his monograph, any local industrial unit run by county, commune, or brigade. He stated that:

> The enterprises may be collectively owned, jointly financed by the state and collective units, or wholly owned by the state but local management. Rural industry also includes units attached to middle schools, hospitals, and health clinics (Sigurdson, 1977, p.1).

In sum, the definition of rural industry that most western scholars used before 1978 equated to industrial units run by counties, communes, or brigades. It therefore included not only collectively owned enterprises, but even those units wholly owned by the state.

From 1978 to 1992, there had been considerable confusion within the Chinese press as to what terms to use to describe rural enterprises. The terms commune and brigade enterprises, village and township enterprises, town and township enterprises, rural enterprises had all been used at various times in various Chinese journals, newspapers and official documents. Officially, the name of 'commune and brigade enterprises' was changed to 'village and town enterprises' in 1984:

> In view of the fact that communes and production brigades will become town and village co-operative economic organizations, many enterprises of a cooperative nature jointly run by some households or by households in different areas as well as many jointly operated and individual enterprises have emerged in recent years. Such enterprises will tend gradually to congregate in small market towns. Therefore, the term 'commune and brigade enterprises' used in the past can no longer reflect the newly developing situation of the enterprises of this category. It is suggested that

6

such enterprises be called 'village and town enterprises' (The Minister of Agriculture, Animal Husbandry and Fishery and the Ministry's Leading Party Group. (1984), *SWB/FE*, 26 March).

In fact, rural enterprises should include private rural enterprises although private enterprises were not legalized until 1988. For example, rural industry in *China's Rural Industry: Structure, Development, and Reform*, edited by William A. Byrd and Lin Qingsong, included private rural enterprises.

Even in the Chinese press, there was confusion over what constituted a rural enterprise with the term 'township and town enterprises' often used interchangeably with 'rural enterprises'. For example, the English language journal, *Beijing Review*, gave the following definition: 'Township enterprises include industries which have been run by communes, production brigades and teams since the establishment of communes. They also included associations of enterprises set up by peasants in recent years, enterprises jointly run by various rural economic sectors and individual enterprises' (Lu Yun, 1984, pp.18-19). However, in the same journal, another article gave the following definition of rural enterprises: 'Rural enterprises are run by townships or towns (The people's communes before 1983), by the villages (previously production brigades), by teams (previously production teams), by several households together or individual households' (Han Baocheng, 1987, p.20). Thus, in essence, rural enterprises and township and town enterprises were the same entities under different names.

For the convenience of this research the author follows the definition of rural enterprises adopted in the Chinese press. Rural enterprises or village and town enterprises include all factories and companies in industry, construction, transport, agriculture, and husbandry, commerce and catering which were operated by towns (townships), villages and individuals. It is important to note that government policy towards rural enterprises was different in terms of ownership structures of rural enterprises. Therefore, in my research, rural enterprises are divided into the following two categories according to the ownership structures of rural enterprises.

The first category is those enterprises originally belonging to communes or large production teams, which now belong to agricultural cooperatives or integrated economic organizations. In some cases, they called themselves 'companies', and were generally administered by rural small town governments. In rural and small town government enterprises, there was often no clear line drawn between government and enterprises. They all bore the clear mark of collective ownership status.

7

The second category comprises the private sector of rural enterprises. These enterprises can themselves be subdivided into two broad areas; private enterprises and individual enterprises. The term 'private enterprises' refers to those whose means of production were privately owned and with eight or more employees (*XHYB*, Vol.6, 1988, p.75), as compared with the category of 'individual enterprises' meaning a business started with private funds with seven or less employees.

Private enterprises were officially classified into the following three types:
(1) Individual investor; (2) Partnership; (3) Limited liability company. Individual investor refers to enterprises managed by a single person. Partnership refers to two or more people who invested as an association, sharing joint management. Limited liability company refers to investors who were responsible to the company for a specific amount, and the company could use the entire amount of its capital to assume the responsibility of the debt of the enterprise.

In addition, most private enterprises had been located in rural areas. The information in 1988 indicated that about 83 percent of the capital funds and labour of private enterprises were located in rural areas. Over 80 per cent of private enterprises were based in the countryside (*NMRB*, 11 July 1988). Therefore, I shall analyze general policy towards individual and private enterprises instead of towards rural private and individual enterprises.

Research hypotheses

This study aims to demonstrate that the main stimulus for the extraordinary growth of rural enterprises from 1978 to 1992 had been the removal of restrictions to their operations. Although the introduction of special programmes and incentives played a beneficial role, they only reinforced the proliferation of rural enterprises resulting from the removal of obstacles to their functioning. As such the main contribution of the reform era had been the creation of a political and economic environment conducive to the expansion of the number, type, and functions of rural enterprises.

After 1976, or more correctly, after Deng Xiaoping took *de facto* control from the quasi-Maoist Hua Guofeng in 1978, the ideological basis of decision making began to change. At the risk of over simplification, the ascendancy to power of Deng Xiaoping marked a shift from 'politics in command' to 'economics in command'. In an attempt to 'catch up' with the industrialized nations of the West and the new industrial powers of Asia (Japan, the Republic of Korea,

Taiwan, and Hong Kong), the social and political revolutions were essentially postponed.

As China was still a backward nation in the early stages of development, it was argued that the development of a modern industrial society had to occur before the transition to communism could take place. Expanding the productive forces therefore increasingly became the base line for any change in society. Whatever helped in economic development, including private and even foreign ownership of the means of production, should not only be tolerated, but actively encouraged. As this study will show, this change in the basic ideological orientation of Chinese decision making had a profound impact on the expansion of rural enterprises, although, as shall be seen, developments had been far from trouble free.

Rural reform was the entry point of the reform program. In an effort to increase rural production, the household production responsibility system was introduced, rural markets were reopened, procurement prices were raised to improve incentives. Without these reforms, the increased agricultural output, rural savings, and rural surplus labour that were a precondition for the development of rural enterprises would not have existed.

Although the removal of restrictions on the role and scope of rural enterprises had been the principal source of their expansion and development, the government had also implemented a number of specific policies aimed at facilitating further developments. These special programmes were primarily targeted at the development of the collective sector of rural enterprises, and had greatly contributed to growth in this area. However, the key element in the considerable growth of the private sector remained the simple tolerance of their existence by a government which previously prohibited their existence.

In addition to policies directly concerned with the expansion of rural enterprises, reforms in other areas of the political economic system had also influenced the scope and nature of developments. Of particular note was the extension of decision making power to local governments, individuals and enterprises; the partial adoption of market mechanisms; a new rural employment strategy; and a regional development strategy based on exploiting regional comparative advantage. In fundamentally altering the underlying political and economic system in China - not least in promoting the acceptance of the legitimate role of market forces and non-state ownership - these policy changes had significantly aided the development of rural enterprises. Indeed, the specific policy changes relating to rural enterprises could not have been implemented without such a reform of the basic structure of the Chinese political economic system.

9

The overall impact of these changes had been the creation of a more relaxed environment and more favourable conditions for the development of rural enterprises. As a result, rural enterprises had developed rapidly. As I have indicated in section one of this chapter, rural enterprises had become a major prop of the rural economy and an important part of the national economy.

However, despite this phenomenal progress, the change of public policy had been inadequate, and many restrictions to the effective functioning of rural enterprises in China remained in place. The old economic structure had been only partially dismantled, and rural enterprises still faced considerable discrimination (whether they were collective run or private run enterprises) in the economic system. This is most clearly evident in official policy regarding access to raw materials and credits, where state owned enterprises received preferential treatments. Rural enterprises had not enjoyed the same competitive position as state enterprises in many other areas such as product transport, retailing and export, and the supply of key production elements. Rural enterprises could not fulfil their true potential within the Chinese economy until these anomalies and restraints on operation were removed.

In addition, some of the special policies designed to facilitate the growth of rural enterprises had been inadequate. Perhaps the best example here was the preferential treatment accorded to rural enterprises in taxation policy, which had been gradually, and prematurely, reduced.

Arguably the greatest challenge to the development of rural enterprises in China had been the fact that despite the dramatic and radical changes in the ideological basis of Chinese decision making in the 1980s, some ideological and political problems still remained. Essentially, not everybody in the Chinese political system shared the belief that rural enterprises were a good thing. On a practical level, some critics had complained, not without justification, that the development of rural enterprises had affected agricultural production, and the development of rural enterprises had polluted the environment. However, even the fundamental ideological question of the acceptability of rural enterprises had not been solved once and for all. Some conservative leaders had expressed concern that the existence and development of private enterprises might lead to private entrepreneurs becoming a distinct class infiltrating the government sector, and could finally result in the restoration of capitalism, which could change the face of socialism and the nature of society in China. Some critics had also warned against the over rapid development of these enterprises, seeing them as a threat to state owned enterprises that would result in a widening disparity between the rich and the poor and between different regions. This suspicion of rural enterprises had been fuelled by accusations that rural

10

enterprises, and especially private enterprises, had been the source of much corruption. These ideological and political problems had been an obstacle restraining rural enterprises' ability to make an even greater development.

Notwithstanding these problems, it should be recognized that both ideological and public policy changes had facilitated a dramatic and rapid expansion in the scope and importance of rural enterprises from 1978 to 1992. Despite the obstacles that remained to their further expansion, the growing social and economic problems, such as rural unemployment, and the economic strength of rural enterprises had pushed against these constraints, and forced the leadership to further reform its public policy, and allowed rural enterprises to play an even greater role in the Chinese economy.

Research method and research plan

My study is primarily concerned with public policy analysis. There are many different definitions of public policy. For example, Eugene J.Kolb (1978, p.285) defined public policy as follows: 'Public policies constitute the expression of a political system's goals and the means with which it pursues them'. Thomas R.Dye (1992, p.2) defined public policy as 'whatever governments choose to do or not to do'. However, one thing is common in that if a policy is regarded as 'public policy' it must to some degree have been generated or at least processed within the framework of governmental procedures, influences and organizations (Hogwood and Gunn, 1984, p.24). Rod Hague, Martin Harrop and Shaun Breslin (1992, p.402) divided the policy process into the following stages: (1) initiation; (2) formulation; (3) implementation; (3) evaluation. Although the decision making process towards rural enterprises is a very interesting issue, the primary purpose of my study is to examine how public policy had influenced the development of rural enterprises as the title of my study has clearly shown. Therefore, my study will mainly deal with policy evaluation. Thomas R.Rye (1992, p.354) thought that 'Policy evaluation is learning about the consequences of public policy'. Peter Jones considered that the evaluation of public policy is concerned to assess the effectiveness and propriety of policy. The narrower approach is concerned to judge a policy only by standards 'internal' to the policy itself, this is, to deal with whether a policy succeeds in achieving its own aims, while the more comprehensive approach would invoke criteria 'external' to the policy, in other words, whether the aims to which a policy is committed are the right ones (Jones, 1992, pp.241-262).

11

In my study, I shall take a comprehensive approach to analyze China's government policy towards rural enterprises. First, I shall make an empirical examination of the policies themselves - the general and specific content of policies. Second, I shall examine the actual or potential consequences of policies, and their immediate and long-range impact on the development of rural enterprises as well as politics and society.

The analysis in this study is primarily concerned with the different central government policies towards rural enterprises. However, in the post-Mao era provincial and lower level authorities had been allowed flexibility in the implementation of central policy. At certain times in certain policy areas, lower level authorities had taken on the function of actually making policy. Therefore, I shall also analyze why regional policy variations had occurred.

My study mainly makes use of information and documents from the Chinese and English press. Party and state leadership speeches, documents and communiques are also important, requiring careful analysis for indications of past and future policy direction. The period during 1978 to 1992 has seen an improvement in information for both outsiders and insiders. During this period, China had established many universities and colleges of finance and economics as well as many research institutes of social sciences at both the national and provincial level. Many journals and books in social science were published in China, while detailed texts of government policies, and mass reaction to some policies, as well as debates over economic questions were more frequently published in national and local periodicals.

Moreover, at the end of April 1980, the PRC was accepted as a member of the International Monetary Fund and the World Bank. As a result, some statistical information has been brought up to internationally acceptable standards. However, China is a developing and socialist country, and some data and information are still lacking. Moreover, some data are misleading. For example, some private rural enterprises registered their businesses as affiliated with collectively owned ones in order to gain the same advantages, while fearing policy changes and discrimination. The recorded amount of private enterprises was thereby reduced.

In the coming chapters, I shall systematically analyze how different policies had influenced the development of rural enterprises from 1978 to 1992. In Chapter Two, I shall discuss the evolution of China's rural enterprise policy. In Chapter Three, I shall deal with local government policy differences towards rural enterprises. In Chapter Four, I shall discuss the implications of market reform and market expansion for rural enterprises. In Chapter Five, I shall concentrate mainly on analyzing the implications of the changes of rural employment and regional development strategies on the development of rural enterprises. In Chapter Six, I shall analyze China's governmental financial and taxation policies towards rural enterprises. In Chapter Seven, I shall examine government policies to improve management in rural enterprises. In Chapter Eight, I shall examine China's government measures to promote technology in rural enterprises. In Chapter Nine I shall draw conclusion, and discuss the implications of China's experience for the former communist countries and developing countries.

2 The evolution of China's rural enterprise policy

In this chapter, I shall explain the evolution of government policy for the development of rural enterprises. I am mainly concerned with the development of rural enterprises from 1978 to 1992. But in order to explain the change in government policy for rural enterprises, a brief review of its pre-1978 policy will be given. Rural enterprises include rural enterprises of both the collective and private sectors. China's policy towards the two sectors had been quite different. Thus, the policy analysis is divided into two parts: the collective sector of rural enterprises and the private sector of rural enterprises.

A brief review of China's policy towards collective rural enterprises before 1978

As early as the 1950s, shortly after the founding of the People's Republic of China, the attitude of China's leadership towards small scale enterprises was either to overlook them, in the haste to build heavy industry, or to focus more on the problem of freeing them from the control of petty capitalists (Kaplan, 1979, p.178). At that time, rural enterprises were underdeveloped. The 'five kinds of artisans' (the carpenter, bricklayer, blacksmith, mason and bamboo stripknitter) and the 'four kinds of mills' (the power mill, bean-noodle mill, oil mill and bean-curd mill) were only predominant in the rural area (Qi Zong, 1982, p.481). Due to the negative attitude of the leadership towards small scale enterprises and to the state monopoly over the purchasing and marketing of grain, cotton and

14

oil, many handicrafts mills were merged, and the 'four kinds of mills' were forced to cease operation because of a shortage of raw materials (Qi Zong, 1982, p.481). ·

China began to enunciate a small scale industry development policy after the people's communes were set up throughout the country in 1958. In addition, decentralization of industrial administration and control functions took place in 1957 and 1958. Small industrial activities throughout the countryside developed very rapidly. By the end of 1958, the labour force in commune run enterprises reached 18 million and the gross output value of these enterprises was over 6 billion yuan (Qi Zong, 1982, p.481).

However, during this period, in order to develop commune run enterprises, the property of the agricultural producers' cooperatives and their members was requisitioned without compensation (Qi Zong, 1982, p.481). In addition, the government also mistakenly promoted many technological processes for which there were no existing small scale options. Large quantities of resources were wasted (Kaplan, 1979, p.180). This kind of 'left' activity caused an agricultural crisis. In order to correct the mistake of depriving the peasants of their property, a policy of 'going bankrupt for repaying debts' was promoted. Therefore, many commune run enterprises were closed. By 1961, the gross output value of commune run industry throughout the country had been reduced to 1.98 billion yuan (Qi Zong, 1982, p.481).

In 1962, the State stipulated that commune and production brigades were not to set up enterprises. As a result, by 1963, the gross output value of commune run industry had further reduced to 410 million yuan (Qi Zong, 1982, p.481). Although rural enterprises had a small increase of their output value, they remained basically stagnant during the following six years (Byrd & Lin Qingsong, 1990, p.10)

During the Cultural Revolution (1966 to 1976), China had adopted the Dazhai Production Brigade in Xiyang County, Shanxi Province as a model to develop agriculture. Some practices of ultra-leftism prevailed. Private plots and domestic sideline occupations of the commune members were all eliminated as 'tails of capitalism'. Commune and brigade industries and sideline occupations were restricted and diversified undertakings strangled. Village fairs were banned. Economic exchange between town and country was stopped. These ultra-left practices associated with the Dazhai Model were promoted across the country, causing great damage to China's agriculture as well as the development of rural enterprises.

However, as Qi Zong indicated, these enterprises had a strong appeal and inspired a great vitality among the people, so they continued to develop (Qi

Zong, 1982, p.482). In addition, China's rural areas began to launch factories to produce agricultural machinery and farm tools for agricultural mechanization during the later part of the Cultural Revolution. Meanwhile, some rural communities took advantage of market shortages because many urban plants had stopped work. As a result, their output value increased from 9.25 billion yuan in 1970 to 27.2 billion yuan in 1976 and 49.3 billion yuan in 1978 (Willian A.Byrd and Lin Qingsong, 1990, p.10).

Therefore, it is clear that rural enterprises had expanded before 1978, though almost entirely in the collective sector of rural industrial enterprises. However, there were the following limitations of policy towards the development of rural enterprises before 1978.

First the attitude of China's leadership towards rural enterprises was to overlook them and to stress their role as the complementarity of agriculture and urban industry. This included two different aspects. On the one hand, rural industry only served as a complement to the modern industrial sector, but on the other hand, rural enterprises also served as a complement to agriculture. Second the market was underdeveloped. It was very difficulty for rural enterprises to buy raw materials in the market. Third, before 1978 China had very strict constraints on farmers engaging in non-agricultural occupations. Under the influence of 'leftist' ideology for many years, the policy of 'grasping grain as the key link' confined a large number of peasants to working a small area of arable land. It condemned 'businessmen' as people 'not engaged in honest work' or even as people 'taking the capitalist road'. Fourth, China did not then allow the development of rural enterprises in the private sector. This will be analyzed in the next section. This also limited the development of rural enterprises. Finally, before 1978 China had not implemented the open door policy. Thus, it was impossible to develop export-oriented rural enterprises.

Policy towards collective rural enterprises from 1978 to 1992

The Maoist version of the centrally planned economy had failed to produce efficient economic growth and had caused China to fall far behind not only the industrialized nations of the West but also the new industrial powers of Asia: Japan, the Republic of Korea, Taiwan, and Hong Kong. In the late 1970s, China's citizens did not have sufficient food and clothing, adequate housing and service sector. Therefore, China's leaders realized that if the Party was to retain its position and the country was not to slide further behind its competitors in terms of economic development, policy changes must take place.

16

In the historic Third Plenary Session of the Eleventh Central Committee of the CCP in December 1978, the party leaders decided to undertake gradual but fundamental economic reforms. China's economic reforms could be distinguished from other reformers like the former Soviet Union and India in two main ways: the open door policy and rural reform policy. The open door policy had provided more opportunities for rural enterprises in China's coastal areas, to gain access to international markets. However, its impact for China's rural enterprises was marginal. The most significant impacts of policy changes for rural enterprises came from rural reform.

The first step in reforming the rural sector was the introduction of the household production responsibility system. Under this system, the cooperative assigned specific plots of land to a family to cultivate for up to fifteen years. For each piece of land, the cooperatives specified the quantity of output that had to be delivered to procurement stations. Any surplus was for the household to dispose of as it saw fit. Families could consume the surplus or sell it on rural markets as they wished. As a result, agricultural output increased rapidly, creating a solid base for the development of rural enterprises.

Second, the government had removed the constraints against farmers engaging in non-agricultural occupations, and had allowed a large number of rural people to go into non-agricultural occupations. Households with insufficient labour were able to transfer land contracts to families that were interested in cultivation and animal husbandry. Peasants were permitted to shift from crop cultivation to commercial, service, construction, and industrial activities in rural enterprises. These reforms had facilitated the supply of surplus labour for rural enterprises.

Third, rural markets were reopened. The rural marketing system changed substantially. Households with marketable surplus had several options: goods could be consumed, sold in local markets, or sold to state stations according to signed purchase contracts. The government also raised procurement prices to improve incentives. These rural reforms had generated the rural savings necessary to develop rural enterprises.

Fourth, reform policies also reduced major administrative barriers that had limited labour and capital from moving beyond commune boundaries. Capital in rural areas was permitted to move across administrative boundaries, and individuals invested not only in their own farm production but also in business ventures outside their own villages. In particular, rural enterprises had been allowed to be established in small towns. These policy changes had provided rural enterprises more chances to be concentrated in small towns and to cooperate with state enterprises.

From 1978 to 1992, the Chinese government had attached great importance to the development of rural enterprises, regarding their development not only as an important facet of readjusting the rural economic structure and a strategic measure to vitalize China's rural economy, but also as the road to the integration of urban and rural areas.

In December 1978, the CCP's 11th Central Committee emphasized at its third plenary session the need to develop commune- and brigade- run enterprises. The Third Plenary Session of the 11th Central Committee of the Communist Party of China pointed out in its 'Decisions on Some Questions Concerning the Acceleration of Agricultural Development':

> Under the principles of reason and economy, all agricultural and sideline products well-suited to being processed in rural areas should be increasingly produced by commune and brigade enterprises. Factories in the cities should, in a planned way, turn over those products or parts which can be processed in rural areas for processing by the commune and brigade enterprises, as well as lend support in equipment and guidance in technology (Ma Hung, 1982, p.140).

Therefore, China's leaders decided that urban enterprises could hand over to commune and brigade enterprises the production of those commodities where processing was suitable in rural areas. As we can see, although this policy change facilitated the expansion of the operations of existing rural enterprises, the CCP was not yet prepared to legitimate the expansion of the non-state sector. At this stage, the notion that the communes and brigades should control affairs remained firm.

In 1980, the campaign to reorganize rural enterprises was launched. Certain enterprises were closed, suspended, merged or transferred. Their number of rural enterprises was reduced from 1.48 million in 1979 to 1.43 million in 1980, but their total income and profits were higher than those of the previous year (Chen Tesheng, 1986).

In order to reduce discrimination against commune and brigade enterprises, the State Council in 1981 issued 'Several Regulations on Commune and Brigade Enterprises in Implementing the Principle of National Economic Readjustment'. In this document, the importance of commune and brigade enterprises was reaffirmed. In 1983 the Central Committee of the CCP further issued 'Several Questions on Current Rural Economic Policies', and called for continuing to consolidate and develop commune and brigade enterprises (Byrd & Lin Qingsong, 1990, pp.10-11).

18

After the household production responsibility system was successfully implemented in agriculture, China's leaders decided to introduce the contract system into commune and brigade enterprises. In March 1983, a *People's Daily* commentator (*RMRB*, 29 March 1983) called for local government to introduce the contract system into commune and brigade enterprises after he summarized the experiences of the Shangquiao Commune in Xuancheng county, Anhui province. He argued that the contract system had enhanced the rationalization of the structure of business management and had changed the situation of stagnation in development; this system had been described as orientating the direction of management toward serving the society and market demand. He also thought that this system had systematized enterprise management, and combined responsibilities, power and profits so that enterprises had power to make management decisions. The implementation of the contract system had aroused the enthusiasm of the workers in production, had thus improved the management of rural enterprises. I shall further discuss this issue in section 7.1 of Chapter Seven.

1984 was a very important year for rural enterprises. The CCP Central Committee and the State Council issued a circular to transmit a 'Report on Creating a New Situation in Commune and Brigade Enterprises' by the Ministry of Agriculture, Animal Husbandry, and the Leading Party Group of the Ministry in March, 1984 (Xinhua in Chinese 07:31 GMT 17 March 1984, *SWB/FE*, 23 March 1984). It argued that China should use diversification as the strategic principle to utilize surplus labour in rural areas so that China could change the situation of having 800 million people producing food and gradually accumulate the large amounts of funds needed to modernize agriculture. In this report, village and town enterprises were considered as an important component of a diversified economy, an important pillar of agricultural production, an important way for the masses of peasants to achieve common prosperity, and an important source of state revenue.

In addition, in this report, the development of village and town enterprises was described as being conducive to expanding agricultural capital construction, increasing the strength of the agricultural co-operative economic organization and providing more and better agricultural machinery and services for peasants. This report argued that the development of village and township enterprises could promote the system of contracting specialized jobs and suitably expanding their scale of operations. Their development could also promote the growth of the market towns, accelerate the construction of economic and cultural centres in the countryside, and prevent peasants who gave up farming from leaving the countryside, and deter the massive influx of peasants into the cities.

Furthermore, in this report, village and town enterprises were regarded as an important force in the national economy and an important supplement to state owned enterprises.

This report is the most important official document concerning rural enterprises published in the 1980s. It can be seen that China's leaders had realized the important roles of rural enterprises in the development of agriculture, solving rural unemployment and the national economy. This report also regarded individual rural enterprises as a part of village and town enterprises, and gave a permit for further development. As a result, this had provided a base for the development of private enterprises. Moreover, this report called for party committees and governments at various levels to give village and town enterprises 'positive guidance' and 'necessary support'. However, in this report, rural enterprises were still asked to play a supplementary role to agriculture and state owned enterprises. At this stage, China's leaders did not realize that rural enterprises would become a serious challenge for state enterprises in the late 1980s.

The CCP Central Committee also supported the development of town and township enterprises in its Documents No.1 and 4 in 1984. It provided policy guidance concerning credit extension and taxation of township and town enterprises in its Document No.1, 1985 (Chen Tesheng, 1986). In its Document No.1, 1986, it claimed that the development of township and town enterprises was of great economic and political significance and urged various departments to adopt supportive measures (*RMRB*, Overseas Edition, 23 February 1986, p.3). The above discussion provides the evidence of the gradual introduction of new policies and measures to promote the development of rural enterprises. It also shows that the central government was aware of the importance of the development of rural enterprises given its wider commitment to agricultural reform. However, it is important to note that at this stage, developing the private sector of rural enterprises was not considered to be a viable option. Indeed, the legalization of private rural enterprises - the first step in their development - did not occur until as late as 1988.

Scholars in China also regarded the emergence and development of township and town enterprises in rural areas as an objective necessity. They believed that to practice a planned commodity economy on the basis of public ownership and to promote socialist commodity production and socialist commodity exchanges, the development of township and town enterprises was inevitable (cf. Ku Sungnien and Yen Yinglung, 1985, p.55). The second stage in China's rural reform had to continue the policies of liberation and invigoration, promote the development of rural productive forces, help the countryside transform itself from a semi-self-sufficient natural economy to a planned commercialized economy, transform traditional agriculture into modernized agriculture and gradually reduce the gaps between industry and agriculture and between city and countryside so that the national economy could develop rapidly and in a balanced fashion. The key to the second stage in rural reform was the vigorous development of township and town enterprises (Lu Xueyi, 1986, p.1). The main arguments for the necessity of the development of rural enterprise were as follows (cf.Huang Shouhong, 1990a, pp.39-46):

Firstly, the financial resources of the State were limited and it would be unrealistic to expect the State to provide more funds to subsidize agricultural modernization. China had to make new breakthroughs in agriculture, it had to introduce new inputs, maintaining and expanding farmland irrigation and drainage systems, promoting greater agricultural mechanization, increasing inputs of quality chemical fertilizers and pesticides and applying and disseminating science and technology, such as developing and spreading improved crop strains. These would require a tremendous amount of funds. With the development of rural enterprises, China could use the profits generated by these enterprises to provide financial assistance to agriculture so as to enable the agricultural sector to continue to develop.

Secondly, the development of rural enterprises could not only support the prosperity of the rural economy, change and reform rural economic structure, but also push the development, change and reform of the national economy, and influence the future of China's economy. On the side of the growth in the economy, rural enterprises could make prominent contributions, manifest in the increase of gross output value, national financial revenues and foreign exchange earnings. The development of rural enterprises could also make contributions to both market supply and market expansion and promote changes in the economic structure at a comparatively fast rate.

Thirdly, in order to achieve rural specialization, China had to change the situation in which the majority of people engaged in agriculture, and the only way to do this was to transfer peasants into non-agricultural employment. It was impossible to accomplish this if China depended on state sponsored secondary and tertiary industry to absorb all surplus rural labour. Thus the way was to let peasants raise their own funds, set up various rural enterprises on their own and transform themselves into enterprise employees. Furthermore, the development of rural enterprises could restructure the irrational mix in China's rural output by developing rural secondary and tertiary industry.

Fourthly, it would be impossible to produce sufficient commodities if over 800 million peasants continued to engage in agriculture. Moreover, China's commercial, communications, storage and shipping and service sectors were too backward and fell far behind the levels attained in China's primary and secondary industries. Thus the mobilization and encouragement of rural enterprises to engage in commercial, transport, service and other industries comprised another important link in the reform of the commercial system.

Compared with China's government policies towards collective rural enterprises before 1978, the government took direct measures to promote collective rural enterprises. Some reform measures to promote management and technology had taken place in the collective sector of rural enterprises. The main reform measures were as follows: Firstly, the 'production responsibility system' and new contractual arrangements were introduced in rural enterprises; Secondly, the labour recruitment system had been changed; Thirdly, a new income distribution system had been introduced; Fourthly, the central government adopted some policies to promote product quality in rural enterprises; Fifthly, the 'Spark Plan' promoting the technological level in rural enterprises was implemented; Sixthly, the central government adopted a more flexible policy to allow technological personnel to work in rural enterprises; Seventhly, the central government had taken some measures to promote technological cooperation between rural enterprises and state enterprises and between rural enterprises and research institutes. These government policies and measures had profound impacts on the development of rural enterprises, which I shall further analyze in Chapter Seven and Chapter Eight.

Furthermore, the State had extended decision making powers to local governments, enterprises and individuals. Local governments had been allowed to adopt different models to develop rural enterprises. I shall further deal with this issue in Chapter Three. Since 1978, China had also engaged in market reform. There had been a considerable development of the market. The reform of the market had made a noteworthy contribution to the development of rural enterprises from 1978 to 1992. I shall analyze their implications in Chapter Four. In addition, the government had changed rural employment and regional development strategies, and had also encouraged the development of rural enterprise by providing favourable tax and financial policies and offering rural enterprises lucrative investment opportunities. I shall examine these issues in Chapter Five and Six.

While central government policy encouraged rural enterprises to coordinate with state enterprises and promote joint ventures during 1980s, it did not encourage activities that competed with state enterprises for energy and raw materials in short supply. That is, rural enterprises were expected to exploit locally available resources and not to increase the use of scarce national resources.

During the early 1980s, rural enterprises played the role of making up for the deficiencies of large enterprises rather than competing with them. However, in the late 1980s, this relation changed, and rural enterprises began to compete with state enterprises for the supply of raw materials. The State's attitude had been to ensure the supply of raw materials to state enterprise, and to allow the remaining or newly increased raw materials to be processed by rural enterprises after state procurement quotas were met.

However, rural enterprises had more decision making power in production and management. They could choose from a variety of flexible management methods according to market needs, arrange their own production, supply, and marketing activities, and budget funds retained for their own use (Liu Shiqiang, 1985, pp. 29-32). Rural enterprises had other advantages which state enterprises lacked: they had an ample supply of cheap labour, and the problem of enterprises, sites was comparatively easy to solve. The other was that rural enterprises had many more rights of autonomous decision making. They were responsible for their profits or losses. Therefore, rural enterprises were more competitive than state enterprises.

In late 1988, overheating of the economy, inflation, widening income differential and corruption took place in China. This led to a period of economic austerity. Faced with an economic crisis and resistance from the conservative forces, rural enterprises became a main target of the economic austerity program. From late 1988 to 1991, the government emphasized the key function to be played by state owned large and medium sized enterprises and adopted a policy where state enterprises were definitely favoured in the acquisition of the capital, energy and raw materials. Rural enterprises faced a serious situation: capital funds were scare, energy sources were insufficient, prices for raw materials went up, and the scope of market shrunk.

In addition, some departments in local governments used the excuse of improvement and rectification to indiscriminately collect fees, and impose fines on enterprises, seriously infringing their legitimate rights and interests and placing an unbearable burden on them (ZGXZQYB, 19 October 1990). As a result, during this period, rural enterprises faced serious difficulties under the austerity programme. Many rural enterprises were closed, merged with others or shifted to other businesses; many employees in rural enterprises had to return to the land.

Local governments put great pressure on the central government. Some scholars also made protests against the central government policy of discriminating against rural enterprises. For example, Yu Guoyao and Yi Yandong wrote that it would not make sense to force the growth rate of the township and town enterprises below that of urban industry (*NYJJWT*, No.10, 1989, pp.22-27). Su Bei (1989, pp.32-34) also indicated: 'We have to make a clear distinction: adjusting is not negating. Adjustments want to achieve a steadier advance and a healthier development for township enterprises'.

Moreover, some rural enterprises had already forged business links with urban industries. These links had been widespread in machine-building and among newly opened enterprises. For example, in 1989, in Zhenjiang City, Jiangsu Province, of the 4.7 billion yuan of industrial output value, roughly 2 billion yuan came from rural enterprises which had varying degree of economic ties with urban industries. 30 per cent of township and town industries had close ties with urban counterparts (*NYJJWT*, No.10, 1989, pp.22-27). Many rural enterprises had become workshops of urban industrial enterprises. This type of business connection had made rural enterprises into an indivisible part of urban industry. Attempting to pressure rural enterprises to preserve state industries would also affect the growth of state enterprises.

In late 1991, the political and economic situation was changed again. Some reform measures had taken place. 'Decision of the CCP Central Committee on Further Strengthening Agriculture and the Work in Rural Areas', adopted by the eighth plenary session of the 13th CCP Central Committee on 29th November 1991, indicated actively developing township and town enterprises was a way to develop rural economy, to increase peasants' income, and to speed up agricultural modernization and national economic development. This document called for carrying through the principle of giving active support to township and town enterprises, making plans for the reasonable development of these enterprises, providing correct guidance to them, and strengthening management of them (*SWB/FE*, 3 January 1992).

In addition, important remarks made by Deng Xiaoping during a tour to the south of China, and the Fifth Session of the Seventh NPC had both certainly promoted further economic reform in early 1992. Some important policies had been formulated to encourage the development of rural enterprises. The State Council also issued a package of new policies to prop up rural enterprises, particularly in inland areas in early 1992 (Zhai Feng, 1992). These measures are summarized as follows:

Firstly, local governments had been asked to set up development funds for rural industries, which usually got little investment from the state budget. State run banks increased loans to help successful rural firms with technological innovations. Key rural enterprises were given aid in term of credit, taxes, energy, raw materials, transportation and the employment of technologists.

Secondly, the government had taken further measures to promote technology in rural enterprises. The government allowed successful rural enterprises to increase their depreciation rates in order to update facilities; and their key projects for improving technology could be listed in local economic plans. More college students were encouraged to work in rural enterprises.

Thirdly, the government adopted the measures to expand the scope of businesses for rural enterprises. Certain rural enterprises were granted rights to deal in foreign trade. The government no longer prohibited rural firms from engaging in wholesale and retail enterprises. Service industry was opened a wide door for rural enterprises.

Fourthly, the government adopted the measures to reduce financial burdens on rural enterprises. Rural enterprises were permitted to retain at least 60 per cent of after tax profits. Poor areas were given more help to develop rural enterprises.

These policies for rural enterprises show that the government continued to provide favourable financial, technological and management policies to promote the development of rural enterprises, and create more business opportunities for rural enterprises. In particular, the policies had paid more attention to the development of rural enterprises in poor rural areas. I shall further analyze government's special policies to develop rural enterprises in central and west regions in Chapter Five.

In summary, the central government had relaxed restrictions on the large-scale expansion of non-agricultural activities by rural communities. Furthermore, the government had formulated some policies to encourage the development of collective rural enterprises from 1978 to 1992.

Policy towards individual and private enterprises

From 1978 to 1992 there had been a dramatic change in policy in the People's Republic of China which had again allowed the establishment of individual and private enterprises. Previously China had eliminated private enterprises in the traditional capitalistic sense, leaving only handicrafts as a supplementary sideline. From 1978 to 1992 both 'private enterprises' and 'individual enterprises' had existed. The essential difference between the two in the Chinese thinking was that the latter was categorized as being owned by the labouring people because the owners still thrived mainly on their own work, while the former was traditionally considered 'capitalist ownership' because owners depended mainly on the employment of wage earners. Since the majority of individual and private enterprises were in rural areas, the government policy towards individual and private enterprises had important impacts on the development of rural enterprises. Thus, in this section, first I shall give a brief review of the policy towards individual and private enterprises before 1978. Then I shall examine the government policy towards individual enterprises from 1978 to 1992. Finally, I shall analyze the government policy towards private enterprises.

A brief review of China's policy towards individual and private enterprises before 1978

The development of the private economy in China can be divided into the following periods before 1978 (Ma Jisen, 1988).

The first period lasted from 1949 to 1953. During this period, the government allowed different sectors of the economy to coexist with the state run sector in the leading position. Individual businesses and private capitalist businesses were developed along with the recovery of the country's economy. There were 7.24 million individual industrialists and businessmen in the country's cities and towns in 1949. By 1953, the number of such enterprises had increased to 8.38 million (Ma Jisen, 1988).

The second period was from 1953 to 1956. In 1953, China stated to engage in the socialist industrialization and socialist transformation of agriculture, handicrafts, and capitalist industry and commerce. By the end of 1956, 95 per cent of small trades people joined cooperative shops, cooperative groups, or took part in joint public-private and state owned enterprises; meanwhile, 96 per cent of individual industrial and commercial people joined handicraft production cooperatives or cooperative groups. The transformation left only about a hundred thousand individuals in industry and commerce who had not joined any cooperative (Ma Jisen, 1988).

The third period was from 1957 to 1965. A 14-grade taxation system based on progressive rates was introduced which taxed the individual businesses heavily, the highest tax rate being 86.8 percent (Ma Jisen, 1988). The income of the individual business people was strictly held at a level which just maintained a simple life. During this period, individual enterprises were still allowed to exist. However, there was the nationwide campaign of setting up people's communes, and the so-called socialist transformation of individual industry and commerce was again intensified. Not only those who had joined cooperatives had to

26

advance to ownership by the whole people, but those remaining individual also had to be transformed. The number of individual businesses again plummeted (Ma Jisen, 1988).

The fourth period was the ten years of the Cultural Revolution from 1966 to 1976, though it actually lasted until 1978. During the Cultural Revolution, individual economy was considered capitalistic and was practically eliminated. Most individual industry and commerce were banned or merged. The results were that state and collective industry and commerce monopolized everything. By 1978, only 140,000 people were in individually owned undertakings throughout the vast country of China, and they were mostly small retailers and repairers (Ma Jisen, 1988). In summary, China's policy towards individual and private enterprises from 1949 to 1978 changed from tolerance to elimination.

Policy towards individual enterprises from 1978 to 1992

In 1979, the State decided to restore and develop individual industry and commerce. The authorities thought that individual enterprises were different from private enterprises, in which the private ownership of the means of production was combined with hired labour and the capitalists made a profit through exploiting the labourers. Under socialism, individual industry and commerce were considered a supplement to socialist industry and commerce. In 1980, at a national work conference on employment, the central authorities pointed out more clearly that it was necessary to develop the individual economy to a proper degree. After that, the State formulated a series of policies to encourage peasants and urban residents to develop tertiary industry. Retired workers were allowed to operate individual shops. Some small shops were leased or contracted for individual operation (Li Yongzeng, 1986, pp. 21-22).

The 1982 Constitution stipulated that: 'The individual economy of urban and rural working people, operated within the limits prescribed by law, is a complement to the socialist public economy. The State protects the lawful rights and interests of the individual economy' (*BR*, No.52, 27 December 1982). Thus, individual enterprises in China were accorded legal status again. This was not only important for the development of individual enterprises, but was also conducive to the subsequent development of private enterprises. When individual enterprises were allowed to develop, many of them employed more than eight employees. In the process, the delineation between 'individual' and 'private' became somewhat blurred - indeed, many of these 'individual enterprises' formally became 'private enterprises' after their legalization in 1988. Thus, without formally tackling the question of whether private

27

enterprises should be allowed to exist and develop, the changes in the 1982 Constitution facilitated the subsequent move towards official and legal acceptance of privately owned rural enterprises. As such, the Constitution marked an important watershed in the removal of the restrictions that hindered the development of rural enterprises in post-Mao China.

In February 1984, the State Council issued some regulations governing individual industry and commerce in rural areas in order to strengthen further the leadership, management and supervision over individual industry and commerce in rural areas (*SWB/FE*, 19 March 1984). The regulations stated that the development of individual industry and commerce in rural areas would play a positive role in promoting commodity production in rural areas, stimulating exchanges of materials between urban and rural areas and putting rural surplus labour to multiple use. Therefore, the government tried to strength its leadership over rural individual enterprises, and also expected rural individual enterprises to play a greater role in rural economic development and solving the problem of rural unemployment.

In China, individual enterprises mainly involved small industries, the handicraft industry, the transport industry, the construction and house maintenance industry, commerce, the catering trade, and other service trades. The number of individual businessmen reached 18 million in 1987, but three-fourths of them were in rural areas (*CD*, 15 December 1987).

In some areas where policies toward the individual economy were carried out more flexibly, the development of the individual economy had greatly exceeded the development of state owned and collective enterprises. Individual business operators did businesses with small capital. In order to survive, they had to pay attention to their business goodwill and service quality. The existence of individual businesses was itself a forceful challenge against egalitarian practice.

However, under the influence of 'Leftist' ideology and policies, a few people in society still held a prejudice against individual business operators because some individual businessmen evaded taxes and often practiced fraud and did not observe trade ethics by harming the consumer's interests.

Although the government laid down policies for encouraging the development of the individual economy, individual business operators still felt that their status was low and they were still despised in society and had no bright future. Thus, they wanted only to make big money in a short time by making use of the opportunities brought about by government policies rather than doing business in an honest manner throughout their lives as individual operators.

State policies toward the individual economy had been unstable, and this had placed obvious pressure on individual business operators. In January 1986 the

State Council promulgated its Provisional Regulations Regarding the Income Tax of Individually Owned Industrial and Commercial Establishments in Town and Country, which implemented a ten-bracket progressive income tax aimed to bring under control the high earning of individual businesses (Zhu Qingfang, 1986, pp.33-40). After paying taxes and administrative fees, individual business operators often had to pay many kinds of mandatory fees and contributions in the names of 'sponsoring' or 'raising funds'. Although some problems still remained, the State's policies towards individual enterprises had become more liberal.

Policy towards private enterprises from 1978 to 1992

The first new private enterprises in China emerged in the early 1980s with the beginning of economic and political reforms. More than 80 per cent of private enterprises were based in the countryside. More than 70 per cent of these private enterprises were operating in more developed rural areas along the coast (*CD*, 15 April 1988). Most people working with the newly formed private enterprises were the surplus labour force in the wake of reforms in the rural economic structure.

A private economy used to be regarded as incompatible with the socialist system in China. According to Marxist-Leninist doctrines, ownership of all means of production in socialist countries should be vested in the State. Before 1988 private economy did not have a definite legal position in China. This can be seen in Article 5 of the 1978 Constitution of the People's Republic of China:

There are mainly two kinds of ownership of means of production in the People's Republic of China at the present stage: socialist ownership by the whole people and socialist collective ownership by the working people.

'Ownership by the whole people' denotes means of production owned by the State; and 'collective ownership by the working people' denotes means of production owned by worker or farmer cooperatives.

Public opinion was, accordingly, divided on the treatment of private enterprises since they were traditionally considered 'capitalist'. The most common complaint against the private economy was that entrepreneurs exploited their workers and created forms of labour capital relations which were incompatible with the Chinese socialist system. It was concluded that the private sector of the economy had distorted the economy and destroyed the national plan since some private enterprises engaged in speculation, price boosting, illicit

29

purchase of raw materials, bribery and corruption involving government cadres and used underhand methods to obtain services from workers in government departments and state owned enterprises. There was also a concern in some areas that the development of private enterprises could lead to the development of social stratification; the rich becoming richer and the poor becoming poorer. Thus, it was suggested that the government should adopt a combination of administration and economic measures to tighten control over the development of private enterprises (cf.Mo Zhen, 1986, pp.7-10).

Others who supported the development of the private economy held that it differed in nature from that which existed in the 1950s except for the private employment of workers. The private economy in the 1950s was a 'national capitalist'[1] economy and signified the indigenous development of capitalism in China. In contrast, the private economy in 1980s served as a supplement to the State and collectively owned economies. Nowadays the private economy was not strong enough to determine the nature of China's society. Its supporters stressed its positive role in promoting the productive forces. They believed that China was in the primary stage of socialism,[2] which was characterized by backward productive forces, reflecting the low degree of industrialization and underdevelopment of the market economy. In particular, the per capita GNP in China still ranked among the lowest in the world. Therefore, China had to focus on developing productive forces (Zhao Ziyang, 1987, p.13). Since private economy can promote production, it had to be encouraged. Moreover, it was argued that the policy to encourage the development of the private economy did not necessarily lead to extremes of wealth. Although it allowed some people to improve their living standards before others, its ultimate objective was to achieve general prosperity more quickly.

Although the Chinese Government officially believed that private enterprises inevitably led to the exploitation of labourers, a moderate development of this sector was considered positive in promoting production, providing employment, making people's life more comfortable and increasing state revenues. The authorities had for some time adopted an ambiguous attitude, while they had not taken the strong measures to prohibit the development of private enterprises.

At the 13th Communist Party Congress in October 1987, former Party General Secretary Zhao Ziyang set an authoritative tone on the controversial subject of private enterprises. In his report, Zhao explained why it should be allowed to develop in China. He stressed that:

Public ownership should remain predominant in the primary stage of socialism. However, other sectors of the economy not under the ownership of the whole people are far from adequately developed. The cooperative, individual, and private sectors of the economy in both urban and rural areas should be encouraged to expand (Zhao Ziyang, 1987, p.13).

Zhao also expected the government to 'formulate policies and enact laws governing the private sector as soon as possible, in order to protect its legitimate interests and to provide it with more effective guidance, supervision and control' (Zhao Ziyang, 1987, p.13). It was the first time that the 'private sector' of the economy formed by private enterprises, had been named in an openly published party document as something positive. In adopting an ideological stance that formally accepted that private enterprise had a legitimate and even progressive role to play within a socialist society, Zhao laid the foundations for the legalization of private rural enterprises in the following year. As such, Zhao's speech marked a crucial change in the ideological orientation of China's economic affairs - even if it was only making *de jure* what had been the *de facto* situation since the decision was taken to expand 'individual' enterprises in the revision of the 1982 Constitution.

Subsequently, at the 7th NPC in April 1988, an amendment on the private economy was added to Article 11 of the Constitution:

The State permits privately owned economic entities to exist and develop within the limits prescribed by the law. The private economy is a complement to the socialist public economy. The State protects the legitimate rights and interests of the private economy while providing the private sector with guidance, supervision and administrative regulation (*XHYB,* Vol.4, 1988, p.37).

For the first time, private enterprises were, in principle, accorded legal status in China.

However, until then there had not been any significant elaboration of law or regulation for private enterprises.[3] Lack of laws and regulations had caused problems and hampered further development of private enterprises. Some entrepreneurs feared that the government would change its current policy of encouraging private enterprise. Some private firms had been found to engage in unlicensed dealing or tax evasion, to lack safety facilities or demand long working hours under poor working conditions. For example, an investigation by the Beijing Municipal People's Government in 1987 revealed that some employers did not have any medical insurance, and more than 80 per cent of employees did not enjoy any kind of medical welfare (cf. *CD*, 22 April 1988, Lu

Yan, 1987, pp. 27-28). On the other hand, there had also been cases of infringement upon the legitimate rights of private enterprises. In many cases, private enterprises had been confronted with excessive tax demands or had experienced difficulty obtaining permits to establish their enterprises. For example, one private entrepreneur said he had to treat the person in charge of issuing the business permits to a dinner in a luxury restaurant before he got his permit to open a restaurant (*CD*, 27 May 1988). Thus, it was in the interest of both the government and private enterprises to stipulate clearly the scope of regulation on private enterprises.

Shortly after the 7th NPC in June 1988, the State Council issued the 'provisional regulations on private economy' and the 'Provisional Regulations on Income Tax of Private Enterprises'. They were the country's first two regulations on operation, management and income taxation for private enterprises.

Although the State had done much to protect the development of private enterprises to date, there was still some discrimination against them in access to loans, tax relief and supplies of materials in short supply. Shanxi provincial government made an investigation of 54 private enterprises. It revealed that these enterprises did not receive the same treatment from the authorities as the collectively owned enterprises. For example, they could not get enough raw materials and fuels, which they therefore had to buy at higher prices from the free market. The monthly interest rates on loans to state owned enterprises were also much lower than to private enterprises.

Since some people in power still believed that private institutions deviated from socialist ideals and should not be encouraged, some government departments tended to 'give special treatment to the collectives, slight the cooperatives, and to squeeze out the individual businesses' (*NYJJWT*, 1987, No.5, pp.58-59). The scope for private enterprises in general was officially restricted. For example, the regulations forbid private enterprises from engaging in the military industry, and from dealing in specified goods under state protection and monopoly such as cultural relics, jewellery, automobiles and civilian explosives.

Even amongst those in the CCP leadership who favoured the existence of private enterprises, there was still a belief that private enterprises should not be allowed unrestricted expansion even if it differed greatly from capitalism in capitalist societies. It had to be subordinated to the dominance of public ownership and subject to the guidance and restrictions of state policies as well as government decrees and regulations on taxation and loans.

In short, although private enterprises had acquired a legal status, they still faced many difficulties and different forms of discrimination.

Conclusion

It is now clear that distinct policy changes for rural enterprises had taken place from 1978 to 1992. Before 1978, China's policy concerning rural enterprises had very much emphasized the development of commune and brigade enterprises, in particular, agricultural product processing enterprises. China's leaders overlooked them and only demanded them to complement agriculture and state enterprises. Furthermore, the market was then underdeveloped. The government also had tight constraints on farmers engaging in non-agricultural occupations, and prohibited the development of individual and private enterprises.

From 1978 to 1992 the most significant policy changes towards rural enterprises appeared to be as follows: First, policy changes permitted peasants to engage in nonagricultural activities. In general, the central government provided a policy that encouraged the development of collective rural enterprises. Second, the Chinese government had legalized both individual and private enterprises. The private sector of rural enterprises had been tolerated. These changes of policy had done much to promote the development of rural enterprises.

However, it must also be recognized that although private enterprises had acquired a legal status, in particular, private enterprises still faced many difficulties and different forms of discrimination. Similarly, there was still considerable discrimination against rural enterprises whether they were collective-run or private-run enterprises such as in the supply of raw materials and credits, compared with the policy towards state owned enterprises. Moreover, the policy changes had been inadequate. Some political and ideological problems had still remained an obstacle restraining rural enterprises to make an even greater development. I shall discussed these problems in the following chapters, especially in Chapter Nine.

In this chapter, I have discussed the evolution of China's central government policies towards rural enterprises. From 1978 to 1992 the different regions had adopted the different development strategies of rural enterprises. Therefore, in the next chapter, I shall examine local governments' development policies for rural enterprises. Since the focus of the research in the next chapter is to exemplify local government development policies and approaches of rural enterprises, much care will be given to the selection of case studies. In the next chapter, the cases of Wenzhou in Zhejiang Province, Wuxi in Jiangsu Province and Nanhai in Guangdong Province will be selected for analysis.

Notes

1   In Chinese terms, 'national capitalist' signified capitalists in colonial and semi-colonial countries being oppressed by imperialists and feudalists. In the socialist transformation stage, they had a two-sided nature: they exploit workers but they could become new socialist men by socialist transformation, see in *Jianming Zhengzhixue Cidian* (Concise Dictionary of Politics), Jilin Peoples Press, Changchun, China, April 1983, pp.213-214.

2   In 25 October 1987, former general secretary of the Communist Party of China, Zhao Ziyang, delivered a report in the 13th CCP National Congress. In this report, Zhao stressed that China is now in the primary stage of socialism. It will be at least 100 years from 1950s, when the socialist transformation of private ownership of the means of production was basically completed, to the time when socialist modernization will have been accomplished. All these years belong to this primary stage (*BR*, Vol.30, No.44, 2-8 November 1987, p.6).

3   Flemming Christiansen demonstrated that private enterprises in China were already secretly legalized in 1983 (Christiansen, 1989, pp.78-91).

34

3 Local governments' policy differences towards rural enterprises

The analysis in this book is primarily concerned with central government policy towards rural enterprises. As shown in chapter two, numerous central directives and initiatives were issued and undertaken from 1978 to 1992 to sponsor the growth of collective rural enterprises. However, private rural enterprises did not receive the same preferential treatment.

But one of the most striking features of China's economic (and to a lesser extent, political) development from 1978 to 1992 had been the degree to which provincial and lower level authorities had been allowed flexibility in the implementation of central policy. At certain times in certain policy areas, lower level authorities had actually gone beyond their formal right to exercise flexibility in policy implementation, and had taken on the function of actually making policy. As such, there had been relatively wide discrepancies between what the centre officially decreed, what actually happened on the ground.

In this chapter, I shall address the issue of divergence between central policy and local actions in relation to the development of rural enterprises from 1978 to 1992. I shall show that despite the plethora of national level pronouncements on the 'correct' path of development, there had been no uniform pattern of policy implementation at a grassroots level. Indeed, the process of defining a 'correct' central policy had in many ways been a reactive process - the centre had distilled a national policy through synthesizing disparate elements of local initiatives.

Having briefly analyzed the wider question of centre-local relations in the post-Mao era, I proceed to assess the importance of five key factors in the evolution of differing local policies towards rural enterprises. These are the growth of local power and the development of rural enterprises; the conflicting approaches of rival central leaders; variations in the desire of local leaders to adhere to central policy; the economic legacy in determining an area level of economic development; and the importance of unique geographical and historical factors of different areas. As there were wide variations of local governments' policies towards rural enterprises in Wenzhou in Zhejiang Province, Wuxi in Jiangsu Province and Nanhai in Guangdong Province, a comparative analysis of their development will provide the case studies for this investigation.

The growth of local power and the development of rural enterprises

The gradual evolution of market reforms from 1978 to 1992 might have gone a long way to eradicating the old 'Stalinist' planning structure, but China was still a long way from possessing a fully functioning market economy. Whilst market reforms had aided the development of rural enterprises, the maintenance of some of the elements of administrative control had continued to obstruct and frustrate rural enterprises.

The changing fiscal and financial relationship between centre and province had been a key determinant of the growth of local economic power. As a result of the combination of a number of factors (Breslin, Chapter 7, 1995), many local governments were all but forced to expand their local revenue base irrespective of whether local strategy conflicted with national economic needs and goals. Developing rural enterprises provided an attractive option for many local governments anxious to increase their local revenue base as initial start-up costs were low, and returns on investment were generated relatively quickly. While the growth of provincialism did facilitate the development of the rural enterprise sector, on the negative side many local governments exercised an overtight control of their local economies. What the local government gave, the local government could also take away. As a result, while rural enterprises prospered when times were good, they often found their access to funds and raw materials quickly reined in when the economy took a downward turn.

Another important change occurred in the structure of the rural political-administrative system from 1978 to 1992 (Wang Huning, 1988a, pp.107-115). There were three main components to these reforms. First, the system of city leadership over counties had been changed. After the Cultural Revolution, the Chinese countryside was basically divided into two - the cities engaged in industry, while their peripheries were engaged an agricultural production. Since 1978, however, the cities had been responsible for local agricultural production as well as industry. This change had brought about a closer working relationship between town and countryside. Secondly, the county (*xian*) political administrative system had been changed. The 1982 Constitution stipulated that a standing committee should be formed in the county people's congress, meaning that all county revolutionary committees were to be replaced by county people's governments. The delegates to the county people's congress were to be elected directly by the voters. Thirdly, since the introduction of the new constitution in late 1982, the central government had reformed rural political structures by substituting new townships and village institutions for the commune, production brigade and team and had redefined the scope of their authority and controls. Township governments and villages' committees had to be directly elected by villagers.

These changes had profound implications for the rural political system as well as on the development of rural enterprises. As the Chinese political economist Wang Huning (1988b) commented: 'if a candidate wants to be elected, he must show that he can satisfy local interests'. In rural areas, achievement in developing rural enterprises had become an important criterion for villagers to judge a candidate for village committees and township governments. Moreover, local leaders could gain numerous more tangible benefits from the successful development of a thriving rural enterprise sector.

The conflicting approaches of rival central leaders

Central leaders' attitudes to reform were an important component in the evolution of rural enterprise policy. For example, Hsu argued convincingly that economic developments were shaped and constrained by the pervading political climate of the time, 'it is primarily the political leaders and their ideology that determines political practices' (Hsu R, 1992, p.2). Although provincial and local leaders did have considerable leeway in policy implementation, the goals and priorities of important central leaders set limits to their actions. For example, the acceptance of an individual and private sector of rural industries was dependent on the ideological interpretations of central leaders, and in particular, of Zhao Ziyang (Wang Zhonghui, 1990, pp.83-98).

Despite the extension of local government power in the 1980s, central leaders had by no means lost total control over the provinces. Although they

37

might be prepared to sanction a relatively high degree of provincial 'flexibility', the extent of central leaders' intervention in local affairs had been variable. There were perhaps two main elements here. Firstly, if the issue at hand was one which had crucial implications for the ideological orientation of the state - if it challenged or questioned basic so-called 'socialist principles' - then central leaders were likely to pay close attention to local initiative. Secondly, if there was conflict between leaders at the centre over the direction of the reform process, then they would concern themselves with local affairs either to promote their ideas, or to rubbish those of opponents. For example, central leaders had frequently identified themselves with particular successful local strategies to prove the wisdom of their view. Deng Xiaoping's support for Zhao Ziyang's agricultural reforms in Sichuan is an important case in point here.

With particular reference to rural enterprises, central leaders' attitude towards the development of private enterprises in Wenzhou provides a good and relatively well documented example. Wenzhou region in Zhejiang Province was the first place where private enterprises came to dominate the local economy. As such, policy implementation and development in Wenzhou had a much wider significance than just another example of local distortion of central policy.

In the late 1970s, Wenzhou was a poor, almost unnoticed region of China. However, in the middle of the 1980s, the output of private and individual industries rose dramatically. By as early as 1985, private traders' proportion of total social retail sales had reached parity with the state sector (Wang Youfen and Li Ning, 1986).

According to the communists ideological justification for reform policies at the time, public ownership had to dominate the economy. As a result, the case of Wenzhou's development became an issue of national concern and debate as it challenged the party's own ideological creed. The main question for discussion was whether the growing proportion of the private economy would affect the leading position of the state economy, and ultimately move China away from a socialist economy and society. Or from a more cynical viewpoint, perhaps we can say that the debate was how to change China's ideological stance to justify the rapid economic development that the private sector in Wenzhou had helped to generate.

In defence of the Wenzhou experiment, Wu Xiang, former deputy director of the Rural Policy Research Centre under the State Council, argued that the overall direction and orientation of China's economy would not be fundamentally affected by isolated events in some areas (cf. Wu Xiang, 1986).

As long as the national economy as a whole was dominated by public ownership, then it could easily accommodate some areas where the private sector was in command. Furthermore, almost all the piece-work products produced by the household industry in Wenzhou were small products which could not affect the dominant position of the state economy. Most products of the household industry were sold in vast rural areas and remote mountainous areas, and supplemented rather than displaced existing industries. The state would still be able to use macroeconomic control methods such as taxes, credit, industrial and commercial administration and so on to influence the overall economic direction.

The public airing of the Wenzhou debate inevitably entailed the participation of central leaders. Indeed, it is inconceivable that this debate would have become public without the prompting of a central leader or leaders anxious to prove a point. It is important to note that at this stage (and at many others) further reform of the Chinese economy was obstructed by opposition from powerful conservative minded leaders. An open debate which would hopefully show to the Chinese people the benefits of private industry would force the hand of the conservative leaders and make it difficult for them to halt the momentum for reform. On the other hand, conservative leaders would hope to highlight the negative impacts in an attempt to influence an alternative public opinion.

The development of private rural enterprises obtained support from a group of influential leaders, including Wan Li (former Vice Premier), Zhao Ziyang (former Premier), Tian Jiyun (Politburo member and former Vice Premier) and Du Runsheng (former Director of Rural Policy Research Centre under the Secretariat of the Central Committee). In particular, Zhao Ziyang, the then prime minister (and thus, ultimately in charge of economic affairs), was Wenzhou's most powerful advocate. His support for Wenzhou was developed in a now typical manner - a personal tour to Wenzhou in December 1985 was followed by praise for what he had found at a central cadres' conference held in Beijing on 6-9 January 1986. Following this public announcement of support from the highest level, Wenzhou was approved as an experimental zone for reform in May, and an experimental Zone Office under the auspices of the Rural Policy Research Centre and the Central Committee Secretariat was established (Parris, 1993, pp.242-263). Further support for the pro-Wenzhou 'lobby' was secured when Wan Li brought Deng Xiaoping into the fold (Liu. A, 1992, pp.696-697).

Despite the array of leaders speaking out for Wenzhou model, many conservative leaders were not prepared to admit defeat. Although it proved

39

difficult to oppose the pro-Wenzhou grouping in 1985, they waited until further problems emerged in the reform process to renew the attack on the dangerous capitalist tendencies in Wenzhou. For example, during the anti-bourgeois liberalization campaign in 1987, Wenzhou was used as an example of the dangers of capitalist restoration. Similarly, after the suppression of the 4th June 'democracy movement' in 1989, a conservative Chinese leader wrote: 'I have long heard that Wenzhou's political power is not in the hands of the Communist Party'. The State Council Research Office responded by dispatching a group to Wenzhou for investigation. This counter-attack was in itself countered when Qiao Shi and Li Ruihuan, Central Committee Political Bureau Standing Committee members of the CCP, separately visited Wenzhou in August and September, and both affirmed its achievements in reform and opening up (Chuang Meng, 1992).

The controversy on Wenzhou had cooled down since Deng Xiaoping paid a visit to south China in early 1992, and called for bolder reforms. Building on Zhao Ziyang's 1987 primary stage of socialism idea, Deng redefined socialism to include the following statement:

> To judge whether an economic measure is socialist or capitalist will depend mainly on whether it will develop productive forces under socialism, enhance national strength and promote the living standards of the people (*BR*, 15 June 1992, pp.4-5).

From this point of view, the development of private rural enterprises in Wenzhou was socialist, and should therefore not only be tolerated, but actively encouraged and emulated across the country.

What this discussion demonstrates is that the acceptance of local initiative and the extent of local power was tempered by the attitude and intervention of central leaders. But conversely, the success of the policy line of particular central leaders was also very much helped (if not dependent on) the successful initiatives of local authorities. Where conflict existed between central and local leaders in China, it was not always between all leaders at the centre and all leaders at the local level.

Variations in the desire of local leaders to adhere to central policy

Although central leaders' attitudes were a crucial determinant of the existence and scope of regional policy variations, local government leaders also played a very important role in regional policy variations. Provincial and lower level authorities had always been in a position to modify and even to distort central policies due to their control over policy implementation. But after 1978, this ability to change the substance of central policy initiatives was expanded with the devolution of more decision making powers (as opposed to policy implementation powers) to provincial level authorities.

Township and village leaders were generally very keen on developing rural enterprises which had become an important component of township and village governments' fiscal considerations. But there were also more tangible benefits to local leaders from developing rural enterprises. Many had partially transferred their political power to economic power by becoming involved in running rural enterprises themselves. Their knowledge, experience, personal contacts, and access to scarce raw materials had ensured that their personal incomes as well as the local government's income had benefited from the development of rural enterprises.

Indeed, in some rich areas, township and village government leaders had been unwilling to accept promotion to the next higher level because of the relatively low government wage scale and the prohibition against higher government cadres' engaging in private business. By contrast, in poorer more backward areas, lower-level community government leaders actively strove for promotion to state cadre status because of the financial advantages resulting from the change in household registration status from rural to urban residency (Byrd and Gelb, 1990, pp.375-376). Thus, perhaps not surprisingly, one of the determinants of how supportive of rural enterprises local leaders were was the benefits that they themselves could expect to gain from their development. This is in turn partially dictated by the economic conditions of their area, an issue that I shall return to later.

Another important factor in the development of local strategies was the ambiguity of central government policies and proclamations. With no clear and authoritative voice coming down from the centre, local leaders were free to interpret central orders in a way that best suited their own priorities. For example, Central Document No. 1 for 1983 gave entrepreneurs approval for private hiring of labour, private purchase of large scale producer goods, and pooling of capital in private investment (*RMRB,* 10 April 1983, pp.1-2). Each owner of a private enterprise in rural areas could employ one or two hands, and a person with special skills could take on no more than five apprentices. But the central government adopted an ambiguous attitude towards employing more people; although it gave no encouragement or publicity to violations of the rules, neither did it take any action to stop or punish them.

This not so much allowed, but forced local leaders to develop firm policy guidelines. In conservative areas such as some parts of rural Hebei, local leaders began harassing local entrepreneurs, and demanding a staffing reduction even though these businesses were expanding and becoming increasingly profitable (Yan Nong, 1983, p.13). In contrast, local leaders in some areas went as far as to provide protection for the development of rural enterprises. One simple way of doing this was to classify private enterprises as 'local collective enterprises' or 'partnership enterprises'. They thus qualified for those advantages developed to encourage the collective sector such as tax breaks.

To return to the case study of Wenzhou, of the 225,000 private enterprises, 110,000 with a total force of 1.76 million, were illicitly registered in this fashion in 1988 (Ma Jisen, 1988). This practice was termed trying to get a 'red hat' meaning trying to make private enterprises appear 'not that bad' according to old ultra-leftist standards. It is worth noting that the local authorities also gained from this practice as entrepreneurs were forced to hand over a portion of their profits to the administrative organizations in return for which they obtained their 'red hats'.

Local leaders had not only exercised flexibility in explaining and implementing central government policy, but they had also made their own policies. Local governments in Wenzhou in Zhejiang Province and Wuxi in Jiangsu Province provide the best examples of how local governments transcended the admittedly ill-defined boundaries between flexibility in policy implementation, and policy making. In Wenzhou, 'the policy adopted by the local governments was to let the market solve various basic problems in economic development' (Huang Xu, 1987, pp.37-38). After the central authorities gave approval for Wenzhou to operate a pilot scheme to test further ways of developing the commodity economy in 1986, Zhejiang Party Committee and Provincial Government of Zhejiang and Municipal Government of Wenzhou drew up the 'Wenzhou Region Pilot Scheme'. This scheme had four distinctive features.

First, it provided for legal guarantees for the rights of ownership and management of private businesses and allowed free, unlimited hiring of labour. Qualifying private businesses might apply for permission to issue shares on the open market. Family businesses, joint enterprises and agricultural trades could work in conjunction with state-owned or collective industries.

Second, the scheme accelerated the reform of state owned and collective industry through adjustment of their ownership structure and business

42

management. Ordinary small scale industries and enterprises were gradually 'restructured, converted, leased, and sold'. Some were turned into collective enterprises; some were leased out to collectives or private operators; and a small proportion were sold off, thus becoming completely privately owned. Enterprises that had been running at a loss over a long period and that had no assets to pay off their debts were to be declared bankrupt, with guarantees being provided for their workers.

Third, the scheme provided gradual price liberalization and the creation of a regional pricing system based on market prices. Three price scales were applied to basic means of subsistence: rationed goods continued to be priced in accordance with practical criteria and governmental regulations; some secondary products were subject to guided pricing, with upper and lower limits being set to curb fluctuation. Other products were regulated by the market. Industrial products of daily use were subject to price liberalization, except for a small number of products subject to state allocation.

Fourth, the scheme proposed the implementation of financial reform and liberation of the capital market. Various forms of financial organizations were developed, including city credit cooperatives, and joint stock cooperative banks. Old-style money lenders might also continue to operate. This scheme not only provided the legal guarantees for the development of private rural enterprises before their formal legalization on a national scale, but also offered more liberal policy for the development of the market. As a result, private rural enterprises had rapidly developed ahead of other regions, and different markets have been established in Wenzhou.

In contrast, the local government in Wuxi formulated an entirely different set of policies. The main characteristic of local government policy for rural enterprises in Wuxi had been to discourage the development of the private sector of rural enterprises and to encourage the development of the traditional collective sector of rural enterprises. Svejnar J and Woo J (1990, p.80) demonstrated that local government in Wuxi had firm leadership over the rural enterprises and stressed the development of industrial collective enterprises. Its strategy was to discourage the development of rural enterprises below the village level and protect the collective sector of rural enterprises as much as possible from competition for human and financial resources. Although private enterprises were tolerated, their development had been restrained by limits on loans, restricted access to inputs, and environmental and other regulations.

A third case study, Nanhai County in Guangdong Province, provided yet a third set of policies. Here, the local government had chosen to encourage a mix of different forms of rural enterprises, rather than emphasizing either the private or the collective sector. During the early 1980s, local government in Nanhai encouraged the development of collective rural enterprises, but local leaders did not discriminate against the development of private rural enterprises (Svejnar J and Woo J, 1990, p.80). After 1978, with the development of the open door policy, the relatives of overseas Chinese started to run their own rural industry supported by foreign capital, equipment, business methods and economic information supplied by their kin. The local government had also established joint ventures with foreign firms (mostly from Hong Kong).

The above three examples show that local governments had taken different policy directions to develop rural enterprises, and they had different roles in developing rural enterprises. However, as the following sections will show, divergence in local policy was not solely dependent on different ideological and policy options of individual leaders.

The economic legacy

The Chinese government had not treated all enterprises equally. The ranking order for preferential government treatment was as follows:

1   state-run enterprises
2   township-run enterprises
3   village-run enterprises
4   private enterprises

Higher ranking enterprises received more preferential treatment and favours from the government, such as loans and better access to raw materials and markets. Some local leaders therefore preferred to support and develop higher ranking enterprises wherever possible. In Wuxi, collective rural enterprises had started to grow in China's old economic system of the 1960s and 1970s. For example, after an intense debate in Wuxi in the early 1970s, county authorities decided not to abandon rural enterprises despite the prevailing political wind at the time. As a result of this political 'incorrectness', rural industrial development in Wuxi was far ahead of that in other counties by the late 1970s (Svejnar J and Woo J, 1990, p.75). Thus, the early development of collective rural enterprises clearly influenced local decision makers in developing a collective rural enterprise policy.

Nanhai County is located in a highly developed and urbanized area. Rural enterprises in Nanhai like Wuxi derived much of their initial technical strength from workers who returned to rural areas in the 1960s and 1970s. Guangzhou provided rural enterprises with opportunities to obtain technical assistance in various ways. Although Nanhai did not have as strong an industrial base as Wuxi, it had greater chances to cooperate with foreign enterprises through joint ventures and processing arrangements. Rural enterprises in Nanhai were on a smaller scale. The collective sector of rural enterprises was weaker and the private sector was stronger than in Wuxi (Svejnar J and Woo J, 1990, p.77).

By way of contrast, local governments in poor regions had many difficulties in developing collective rural enterprises since poor regions received less state investment and lacked economic strength. Therefore, if local leaders in poor regions wanted to develop rural enterprises, they had to adopt more 'liberal' policies to encourage peasants to establish their own businesses. This brings me back to the Wenzhou region.

Wenzhou is situated opposite Taiwan across the Taiwan Strait. It was on the 'frontline' in the 1950s when the situation between Taiwan and the Mainland was tense. It was also the site of some of the fiercest conflict during the 'Cultural Revolution' when various Red Guard factions fought pitched battles with guns and artillery. The local economy remained relatively stagnant.

In Wenzhou the industrial and geographical conditions were not conducive to supporting large sized enterprises. In the 30 years between 1949 and 1980, this area's total agricultural output value increased at an average annual rate of 4.9 per cent, which was 0.5 per cent lower than the national average for the same period (Huang Xu, 1987, pp.37-38). In sum, the Wenzhou area had a poor basis in its collective economy, but there were more people than the land could support, and from 1949 to 1978 there was limited investment in capital construction.

The relatively underdeveloped state of Wenzhou's economy went a long way to explaining why local leaders were willing to tolerate and even support private enterprises. In general, rural enterprises in Wenzhou were small scale. They needed little investment since the cost of household industry was low. Most of the production units were labour intensive handicraft and semi-mechanized operations, producing small and medium-sized commodities. They tended to produce small, low price goods which urban enterprises found unprofitable to produce, and they depended on the process of self-accumulation to run their private enterprises.

Since Wenzhou had a lower level of economic development and little investment from the state, local government was not able to rely on collective economic strength to develop collective enterprises, and had little choice but to tolerate and even support the development of private rural enterprises. Thus, the contrasting economic legacies in Wenzhou, and Wuxi had clear implications for the development of rural enterprises in these areas.

Geographical and historical factors

For many scholars in China, the key element in determining the type of local government policy adopted to encourage rural enterprises was the degree of geographic isolation of that area (Liu Yia-ling, 1992, p.300). For example, they argued that local governments in geographically isolated areas received less interference from the central government. As a result, policies that deviate (or even contradict) official central policy were more likely to remain unchallenged in these peripheral areas. It is true that Wenzhou in particular had faced geographic isolation. However, this argument is not convincing since private enterprises had not been developed in many other geographically isolated areas. In fact, geographically isolated regions had disadvantages in securing capital and technical support from big industrial cities, and had also difficulties of access to the market. Therefore, the factor of geographic isolation could become an obstacle to the development of rural enterprises. Furthermore, as we had already seen above, Wenzhou's isolation did not prevent it from receiving very close central government attention in the mid and late 1980s.

Since state owned businesses and supply and marketing cooperatives did not take responsibility for rural enterprises' purchases of raw materials and selling their products, rural enterprise had to rely on their own initiative. In particular, rural enterprises in geographically isolated areas had to rely on procurement and distribution personnel to sell their own products. Whether the region had enough talented people to purchase materials and sell products had thus been a crucial determinant of success and failure for many rural enterprises.

For example, although Wenzhou is located in the mountainous areas, people in Wenzhou have a long entrepreneurial tradition. Indeed, Wenzhou people were known throughout China as the scissors, the razors and the kitchen knives, reflecting the local skill in tailoring, hairdressing and cooking. Before liberation, the peasants worked partly in the fields, partly in family handicraft work, and partly in business. Even in the years of the 'Cultural Revolution', they engaged in business activity, sometimes publicly, sometimes underground. Business tradition had been a very important factor for the development of private rural enterprises in Wenzhou.

Private enterprises in Wenzhou were characterized by distant purchases and distant sales and belonged to the category of small commodity production which was neither closely linked with agriculture nor closely linked with the local economy. The products were mainly sold in distant remote cities and towns. Selling and purchasing agents were scattered around the places of origin of products, and were linked with national specialist markets which were part of an emerging national commercial network. For example, in Liushi township in Wenzhou, the development process consisted of four steps (Qiu Jian, 1988). First, more than 1,300 sales people went into remote areas, selling their products in factories and mines that other sellers had rarely visited. Second, they paid close attention to the different orders at each annual national machinery and electrical products fair. Third, they tried to reduce prices through reducing production costs by making use of scrap materials from big factories to produce small commodities. Fourth, they cooperated with colleagues in Shanghai, Guangzhou, Hangzhou and other cities, making use of their larger counterparts' technology and selling some of their products through these enterprises.

Moreover, some collection and distribution markets for nationally known small commodities had appeared in Wenzhou. In 1986 in the urban and rural areas of the whole of Wenzhou, there were nearly 400 markets, among which 113 were specialized markets. The most outstanding markets were the 10 big, well-known, nationwide specialized markets (Wu Xiang, 1986). The market liaison basis was on households that specialized in buying and selling, involving 100,000 peasants who travelled all over the country to big and medium-sized cities and remote and backward places to buy raw materials, sell products, sign contracts and pass on information (Wu Xiang, 1986).

Therefore, although Wenzhou region faced geographic isolation, people in Wenzhou not only had a long business tradition, but more importantly, they had established effective market networks so that private enterprises could develop in spite of their geographic isolation. Although many mountainous and minority regions in western and central areas also faced geographic isolation, private rural enterprises had not developed since these regions lacked talented marketing staff, and the entrepreneurial spirit shown by Wenzhou's political and business leaders.

In geographical terms, Wuxi in Jiangsu Province is mostly scattered around large and middle sized cities. Rural enterprises can receive capital and technical support from these cities, and can also access this large urban market. Moreover, in Wuxi Jiangsu Province there was an ancestral relation between the cities and rural areas. Those town people who returned to rural areas brought with them not only their technical and management skills but also their networks of social connections, which were essential in obtaining market information and other assistance. Those urban people were likely the initiators in running rural enterprises.

Nanhai county is located in a highly developed and urbanized area about 20 kilometers from Guangzhou City. The agriculture produces enough to support its own population and to export a substantial quantity of products to Hong Kong. There were many small factories in the area before 1949, but the industrial base was much smaller than in Wuxi (Svejnar J and Woo J, 1990, p.75). The rural areas benefited from the return of skilled workers who began to set up their own factories in the countryside. Throughout history, many local people travelled and lived abroad. The overseas Chinese could bring back overseas remittance and foreign capital as well as market information and management knowledge.

Therefore, both Wuxi and Nanhai have the conditions to develop collective rural enterprises since they have good geographic conditions and an ancestral relation with the cities. Moreover, Nanhai County is close to Hong Kong, and has many overseas Chinese connections.

Conclusion

The above analysis has displayed considerable variations in local governments' policies towards the development of rural enterprises. The support of central leaders had been the single most important factor which determined the scope and extent to which these policy variations could exist and develop. However, other factors such as the changes of the central-local relations, financial incentives for local leaders, local economic legacy, geographic and historical factors, had also influenced the existence and development of regional policy variations towards the development of rural enterprises.

Regional policy variations had important implications for the development of rural enterprises. Although some regions had a weak economic foundation and geographic isolation, rural enterprises had nonetheless been able to flourish in these regions. Private enterprises began to dominate state enterprises, and the ownership structure of the area fundamentally changed.

The emergence of regional policy variations towards the development of rural enterprises could reduce regional development imbalance of rural enterprises. As Lin Qingsong (1990, pp.174-175) demonstrated, in the first few years after 1978 the government depended almost solely on collective rural enterprises to develop rural industrialization. The gap among regions had widened alarmingly since a few relatively developed areas enjoyed industrialization while the backward areas were unable to develop collective rural enterprises. Since 1984 the blossoming of private enterprises had helped narrow the gaps, and had offered new hope for solving the problem of regional imbalances.

Moreover, regional policy variations had also produced political implications. The development of rural enterprises in Wenzhou had caused national debate concerning the role of private enterprises. This had facilitated the legalization of private enterprises in China.

The experience of developing private enterprises in Wenzhou had undoubtedly become a challenge to state enterprises. But it also acted as a spur to improve management methods in state enterprises and to deepen reform further. In July, 1986, the 'Regulations on Enlivening State Owned Enterprises' were promulgated by the Wenzhou municipal government (Wang Youfen and Li Ning, 1986). Aimed at extending the decision making power of enterprises, it stipulated that the total wage bill of a profitable enterprise could fluctuate in line with its profits after tax, and an enterprise might allocate those wages in whatever form it chose. Moreover, a loss making enterprise might be allowed limited losses, beyond which no more subsidies could be given by the government. But if the enterprise lost less than the full amount permitted, it might keep the full subsidy. Poorly run or less profitable enterprises could be leased or contracted to individuals or collectives or could be operated as shareholding co-operatives on a trial basis with the approval of the city government.

Therefore, the development of private rural enterprises had not only become a challenge to the state economy, but it had also forced state enterprises to improve their management methods. The development of private enterprises had formed a strong political force. For example, in January 1989 in Wenzhou, 78 successful entrepreneurs established the People Run Business Association (*minying gonghui*). Moreover, one-quarter of association members were also party members (Parris K, 1993, p.261). Therefore, private entrepreneurs had represented a political force within the Party itself, a move

49

that may have significant long term consequences for the future of China's politics.

From 1978 to 1992, China had undertaken fundamental economic reform -- from the centrally planned economy to market economy. The development of rural enterprises had highly depended on the market. Therefore, in the next chapter, I shall discuss the implications of the measures of market reform and market expansion for rural enterprises.

4 Implications of market reform and market expansion for rural enterprises

In Chapter Three, I have discussed local government's policy differences towards rural enterprises. In this chapter, I shall examine the implications of market reform and market expansion for rural enterprises. From 1978 to 1992, China's economy could be divided into a planned and a non-planned sector. China's rural enterprises had highly depended on the market. The reform of the market had played a critical role in the development of rural enterprises. In this chapter, I do not intend to work out why China carried out the reform of the market and what kinds of the measures of market reform should take place in the future. My main intention in this chapter is to analyze how the measures of market reform and market expansion had influenced the development of rural enterprises from 1978 to 1992, and examine some characteristics of the market's use of rural enterprises. First I shall analyze the implications of the measures of market reform for rural enterprises. Secondly I shall deal with the implications of market expansion for rural enterprises. Finally I shall examine some characteristics of the use of the market by rural enterprises.

Implications of the measures of market reform for rural enterprises

After 1949, China adopted a centrally planned command economy. Although the experience of the Soviet Union provided the basic model for this economic system, it marked a separate and distinct economic model from its Soviet counterpart. This system created a strict rationing system for key consumer goods for the entire population and the direct allocation of raw materials and

51

capital goods for enterprises. The system kept the aggregate demand and supply of basic consumer goods under government administrative control, thus making it feasible to guarantee minimum subsistence levels to most people and to achieve artificial price stability.

This system was particularly harmful to the development of rural enterprises. First, under this system, all raw materials and important production means were distributed by the state. The priority of the supply of these materials was given to the state enterprises. Rural enterprises hardly obtained raw materials and energy from the state. Second, under this system, different markets such as information markets and financial markets did not exist, making it very difficult for rural enterprises to obtain the information and funds. Third, under the provisional measures for rationed supply of grain for city and town people, people who wished to transfer their domicile or to add a member to their family had to present their household registration book and credentials for permission; when people changed jobs, they had to present a certificate from the labour department in order to transfer their household registration; when personnel settled in the townships, their household registration and grain coupons were transferred to the place where they settled. They had to get permission, or they would lose their rations. Thus, the system controlled migration of technological personnel to rural enterprises and enforced labour assignments.

After the December 1978 3rd Plenum of the 11th Party Committee, China engaged in a series of market reforms. I shall discuss the implications of these market reforms within the following periods (cf. Prybyla, 1989, pp.1-18, and Liu Guoguan, 1989, pp.22-29): (a) October 1979 to October 1984; (b) October 1984 to late 1988; (c) late 1988 to 1991; (d) 1991 to early 1992. Then, I shall analyze the implications of the measures of market reform towards the development of rural enterprises according to above different periods.

From December 1978 to October 1984

During this period, the following reform measures were introduced: First, the household contract responsibility system was implemented in rural areas, thus providing farmers with incentive for work. As a result, agricultural output increased. This offered two bases for the development of rural enterprises. First, it provided a sufficient supply of grain for farmers to engage in rural enterprises. Second, a considerable proportion of farmers became surplus. This provided a sufficient supply of labour for rural enterprises.

Second, the state's monopoly on the purchase and marketing of agricultural products was reduced. By 1984, the number of agricultural commodities subject to compulsory state procurement had been reduced from 29 to 10 (Prybyla, 1989, p.1). In addition, agricultural price reforms had increased payments for compulsory deliveries of agricultural products and raised rural income. Higher incomes had led to increase rural demand for consumer and producer goods, though the quantities supplied had been insufficient (Sicular, 1985, pp.108-109). Thus, this created a demand market of consumer goods for the development of rural enterprises.

Although price reforms such as adjustment of ex-factory prices throughout industry and reform of the existing price management by abolishing 'pricing-fixing by directive' were recommended during the period 1980 to 1981, the plan for general price reform was not put into effect (Wu Jinglian and Zhao Renwei, 1988, p.21). Thus, the reform of the market was limited during this period.

From October 1984 to late 1988

In 1984 the political and economic atmosphere shifted to favour more radical reform. Therefore, some reforms of the market took place.

During this period, the most important reform of the market was the implementation of the dual pricing system. The decision of the State Council, in May 1984, 'On further Expansion of Decision Making Power on the Part of State Run Industrial Enterprises', stipulated that there were in the planned economy and the non-planned economy, two types of material supplies for the enterprises, namely, state allocation and free purchase by individual enterprises; and the prices of the goods produced outside the state quota system could be varied within a range up to 20 per cent higher or lower than state prices. In February 1985, the State Price Administration and the State Material Administration jointly cancelled the 20 per cent limit (Wu Jinglian and Zhao Renwei, 1988, p.22). The dual pricing system had very important implications for the development of rural enterprises.

Since industrial enterprises that formerly had to obey government production directives had been given more freedom to produce products they could dispose of them at prices set by themselves. Thus, they had a great incentive to seek markets and profit. As a result, rural enterprises could buy more raw materials and some products from the market. The market environment was thus much improved for rural enterprises.

However, since there were the shortages of raw materials and funds, competition existed between rural enterprises and those owned by governments at county, provincial and central levels. Rural enterprises had an inferior competitive position compared with government run enterprises at higher levels.

The former had relied mainly on the market for everything they needed, the latter had been more or less guaranteed by the State a supply of production materials, advanced technology and professional people. Moreover, their products enjoyed easier access to the market due to their firmly established sales channels and information networks. These unfair conditions forced rural enterprises to pay a high price for their survival and development.

The dual pricing system also created an opportunity for producers and commercial intermediaries. Certain people with official positions or personal connections could use ties of friendship, and the power to give orders, to grab illegal profits. This was mainly because industrial growth had outstripped intermediate level support, causing bottlenecks to emerge in the supplies of coal, electricity, and transport facilities. The prices of consumer goods and raw materials on the free market were always double or triple the planned prices. In order to survive, rural enterprises had to depend on favours and gifts in order to obtain raw materials and sell their goods and get loans. However, these illegal activities were very unpopular, and the dual price system was criticized for facilitating them. These (and other) irrationalities in the economic system also contributed to economic and social disorder during the summer of 1988, with a series of bank runs and uncontrollable panic buying in some cities (cf. Li Wei, 1988).

From 1978 to 1992, China adopted an open door policy. There were four Special Economic Zones, 14 port cities and three river deltas in Guangdong and Fujian provinces and around Shanghai which enjoy special privileges in order to encourage their economic development and by opening them to the outside world. In addition, the State decided to turn Hainan Island into the country's largest special economic zone and to extend more open policies in the pilot provinces of Guangdong and Fujian. China's rural enterprises were also linked with foreign trade. Although the first step linking the rural areas to foreign trade in the post-Mao era was started in 1978 in Guangdong, the first nation-wide effort to link the rural economy with the export sector occurred in 1984 (Zweig, 1991, p.721). As David Zweig pointed out, Zhao wanted to restructure agricultural production to meet the needs of export markets. However, at this time Zhao's strategy was still limited to particular rural export bases, not extended to the whole of the countryside (Zweig, 1991, pp.721-722).

In 1987 Wang Jian in the State Planning Commission proposed a world market-oriented economic development strategy for China's coastal areas. In this strategy he suggested that rural enterprises should play an important role in the labour intensive export economy. In 1988 China adopted the world market-oriented economy development strategy for China's coastal areas. According to this strategy, China's coastal areas, which cover 320,000 square km and have a population of 160 million, introduced flexible preferential policies to attract more foreign funds and technology, and further expand foreign trade and economic exchange (Han Baocheng, 1988, p.16).

The main arguments in favour of coastal areas' development strategies and the development of rural export-oriented enterprises were as follows (cf. *BR*, 8-14 February 1988): there was ample cheap labour in the country's coastal areas to assist in the development of labour intensive products which still made up a comparatively large part of the world markets. Coastal areas had the advantages of cheap labour and a highly skilled workforce, better industrial facilities, more capability of scientific and technological studies and convenient transport compared with other developing nations. With independent decision making powers and flexible management methods, rural enterprises could easily adopt to the ever changing international market. In addition, rural enterprises could make full use of local resources to reduce processing costs and improve competitiveness of the products for export.

During this period, rural enterprises had been the most important growth sector of foreign trade. For example, in eastern China, there were about 35,000 township and town enterprises, employing nearly 3 million employees, earning foreign exchange. From 1984 to 1989, township and town enterprises accumulated a total of 20 billion US dollars in foreign exchange earning for the state. In 1989, foreign trade purchases from township and town enterprises in eastern China amounted to 22.9 billion yuan, accounting for 30 per cent of all foreign trade purchases in eastern China (Huang Shouhong, 1990b). The open door policy and the world market-oriented economic development strategy for China's coastal areas had encouraged rural enterprises to develop an export-oriented economy, and had made it possible for rural enterprises to access international markets.

This period also witnessed a considerable decentralization of economic administrative control and liberal policy towards the development of rural enterprises. This resulted in rapid growth of rural enterprises. From 1986 to 1988, rural enterprises increased at an average annual growth rate of 38 per cent (*LW*, No.52, 30 December 1991).

However, although grain output peaked in 1984, further grain production stagnated. Moreover, after the reform of the urban industrial sector in October 1984, the urban industrial economy had become extremely resistant to structural change in two areas: prices and property relationships. In addition, there was a weakening of the instrumentalities of central administrative command planning, there was no corresponding adequate strengthening of market instrumentalities of information, coordination, and incentives. As a result, there was overheating of the economy, inflation, widening income differentials, and corruption (Prybyla, 1989, pp.3-6). This led to the third stage, from 1988 to 1991, a period of austerity

From late 1988 to early 1991

Faced with economic crisis and resistance by conservative forces, the government postponed further price liberation and, in late 1988, adopted a series of austerity policies. The authorities introduced administrative guidelines to reduce state investment in 1989 by 20 per cent and to cancel or defer a large number of projects in low priority sectors such as services, office construction and processing industries (The World Bank, 1990). There was a marked slackening in the rate of industrial growth through 1989, which became negative in the last quarter. By the first quarter of 1990, industrial output regained lost ground and was at the same level as a year earlier (The World Bank, 1990). As a result, urban unemployment had worsened, and the large number of rural migrants had returned to the countryside.

A contradictory monetary policy, relying principally on the administrative allocation of credit, was imposed. For example, the People's Bank of China set a target of 15 per cent for the growth of credit in 1989 and began stringently monitoring changes in credit supply (The World Bank, 1990). During that period, state loans for rural enterprises reduced rapidly. Former Agricultural Minister He Kang asked rural enterprises to rely on their own funds to compensate for the reduction of bank credit and to practise thrift and cut unnecessary capital construction during the austerity period (*BR*, 22-28 January, 1990).

In addition, direct control on prices and marketing was introduced in late 1988. For example, local governments were required to notify the central authorities whenever they raised prices for a range of daily necessities and certain raw materials. The wage bill of the urban formal sector was frozen until the last quarter of 1989 (The World Bank, 1990). Rural enterprises faced severe shortages of raw and semifinished materials, particularly iron and steel materials as well as increased prices. For example, the price of coal rose from 130 yuan per ton at the beginning of 1988 to its 1989 price of 250 to 300 yuan per ton. Because of a lack of coal, the amount of electricity being generated by power plants suddenly declined. For example, a major power plant in Jiangsu, the Jianbi Power Plant with an installed capacity of 1.6 million kilowatts, in January 1989 only produced 500,000 kilowatts. The negotiated price of electricity had increased from 40 yuan per kilowatt-hour in 1988 to 65 yuan per kilowatt-hour in 1989. Since negotiated price electricity only supplied a portion of enterprise needs, more and more enterprises were buying diesel generators, and because of the increased number of plants using them, the price of diesel oil was pushed up. It rose from 1,200 yuan per ton in 1988 to 1,800-2,000 per ton in 1989. The price of raw and processed materials also greatly increased (Yu Guoyao and Li Yandong, 1989, pp.22-27).

During this period, rural enterprises faced serious difficulties under the austerity programme. More than 3 million companies were shut down, merged with others or shifted to other businesses in 1989, and 8 million employees had to return to the land (*BR*, 22-28 January 1990, pp.28-29).

From early 1991 to early 1992

After 1991, government policies had turned reformists again. The reform of the market continued. In January 1991 the remaining export subsidy was abolished, and a series of micro-devaluations of the yuan was begun (*TE*, 1 June 1991). On 1 May 1991, the Chinese government greatly increased the sale price of grain and edible oil, prices which had stayed unchanged for 25 years (1966-91) (Niu Genying, 1991, pp.11-2-14). In addition, the government also raised prices for railway transportation, crude oil and steel products. These price adjustment were designed to eliminate the distorted price structure (Niu Genying, 1991, pp.11-2-14).

Reform of the financial market included establishment of a money market, including bond and stocks markets, both short-term and long-term. For example, the exchange rate of RMB was slightly adjusted and the value of RMB reduced so that the official and market exchange rates were basically in balance. The interest rate for savings deposits was reduced on average by one percentage point and interest rates for loans by 0.7 percentage point (Niu Genying, 1991, pp.11-2-14). Some 25 per cent of the state treasury bonds were purchased and sold exclusively by other financial organizations with satisfactory results. With approval of the State Council, the pilot shareholding system was further expanded in Shanghai and Shenzhen (Niu Genying, 1991, pp.11-2-14).

These reform measures were successful. For example, after price adjustment of grain and edible oil took place, except for a few cities where residents queued up to buy grain and oil for a short period of time, the grain and oil market was stable and no panic buying similar to that which occurred in 1988 took place (Niu Genying, 1991, pp.11-2-14). Further market reform had given rural enterprises even more opportunities to gain access to different markets.

However, they had also faced an increasingly competitive market environment putting great pressure on them to perform well. This environment had undoubtedly continued to increase the efficiency and flexibility of rural enterprises.

To summarize, from 1978 to 1992, China had engaged in a series of market reforms. In the process of these reforms, the scope of the mandatory plans had been reduced and the scope of the guidance plans extended. Other economic activities were regulated partly or entirely by market adjustment in accordance with their respective circumstances. A nationwide survey made by the State Planning Commission in 1989 found that the mandatory plans covered 17 per cent of the nation's industrial production; the guidance plans of various departments of the State Council, various provinces and cities, 43 per cent; and market regulation, 40 per cent (*BR*, 28 May - 3 June 1990). As a result, the Chinese system of material allocation had become more decentralized. Even such key products as coal and steel were produced in enterprises at both central and lower levels of control and were allocated through largely separate and self-contained channels. These reforms were vital for rural enterprises to survive and develop. Although China's market system had not been perfect, it cannot be denied that the reform of the market had made a noteworthy contribution to the outstanding development that had taken place among enterprises from 1978 to 1992.

Implications of market expansion for rural enterprises

The expansion of the market had created many opportunities for the entry of rural enterprises into the market economy. From 1978 to 1992, the extent of rural and urban markets had undergone a remarkable development. The number of free markets increased from 33,302 in 1978 to 79,188 in 1992. The value of trade in the market increased from 12.50 billion yuan in 1978 to 353 billion yuan in 1992 (*China Statistical Yearbook (1985)*, p.477, and *China Statistical Yearbook (1994)*, p.499).

China had also set up a variety of markets until 1992. For example, China then had more than 800 trading centres for daily necessities, 239 wholesale markets for small industrial products, 1,267 wholesale markets for agricultural and sideline products, 72,000 urban and rural free markets and more than 400 markets for means of production (Wen Tianshen, 1992, pp.14-17). Many labour exchanges, science and technology markets and financial markets had also come into being (Wen Tianshen, 1992, pp.14-17).

The markets for means of production, consumer goods, technology, information, labour services, real estate, etc. had expanded in different degrees in different regions. Nevertheless, several general patterns could be distinguished. First, the country's consumer goods market's growth was at a more mature stage, with most of the commodity items already liberalized. The number of commodity items directly controlled by the government dropped from 55 in 1978 to 22 in 1986. The number of agricultural by-products whose prices were directly set by the government, had also been lowered from 113 items to 25, accounting for an estimated 30 per cent of total sales, the other 70 per cent being sold at prices following government guide lines or market-adjusted prices (*ICM*, January 1988, p.9). State dictated prices on industrial commodities had likewise been limited to items which totalled merely 40 per cent. Pricing of more than 1,000 small commodities was gradually liberalized (*ICM*, January 1988, p.9).

In the 1980s the Chinese people's consumption erupted into what economists called an unprecedented spending spree: electrical household appliances, expensive home furnishings, and fine clothing quickly became part of the everyday life of the average Chinese family. China's urban enterprises had not taken time to complete the necessary process of structural adjustments to this consumer boom, and this created a perfect opportunity for rural enterprises. At the same time, traditional heavy industries made the transition to light industries, and the production of small volumes of a large variety of parts and components opened more doors for rural enterprises. Therefore, the emergence and expansion of the commodity markets had created enormous business opportunities for rural enterprises.

Second, a market in materials of production gradually began to emerge. By 1986 the market dependent share of steel products reached 45 per cent. Pig iron reached 53 per cent. Soda ash and caustic soda reached 55 per cent and 31 per cent, respectively (*ICM*, January 1988, p.9). This indicated considerable success for the market dependent system in the circulation of materials of production. Essential materials of production used to be uniformly rationed by the State. After an enterprise fulfilled the plan of commodity production set by uniform regulations, all additional products could be sold for their own benefit. For example, rolled steel was sold at two different prices. The state-set price for one ton was 700 yuan while the market price was up to 1,400 yuan (*CD*, 6 October 1988). In general, the free market price was much higher than the state price, and this had encouraged enterprises to produce and sell more materials in the market. As a result, more materials were available in the market.

One survey (Du Haiyan, 1988, pp.21-32) shows that although rural enterprises, mainly collective rural enterprises, also became eligible for the supply of planned allocated materials as part of the reform of the materials supply system, the supplied materials did not amount to as much as one percentage of rural enterprise's total materials consumed. Thus, the reform of the market benefited rural enterprises. The opening of markets for the means of production reduced their difficulties in getting materials. Other survey (Du Haiyan, 1988, pp.21-32) shows prices of materials distributed by county and rural governments were oriented to markets since most of the materials distributed by county and rural governments were purchased from markets. In some cases, materials bought from markets were bundled together and distributed together with materials purchased under plan at parity price. As a result, the price of distributed materials was either the market price or close to the market price.

However, the proportion of materials of production provided by planning systems differed for different business categories. In general, for most medium-to-big businesses planned distribution had a larger share while for small businesses it had a relatively small one, or none at all. This unequal competition among businesses differed in terms of investment and production, and limited the efficiency of the market dependent system. The disparity and imbalance in their reliance on the market for materials of production market also weakened the system's effectiveness in regulating production and circulating commodities.

Another problem that existed in the materials of production market was that reselling became a rampant practice due to insufficient supply. This not only triggered blind development of some commodity businesses, multiplied the distribution for some means of production, and enlarged distribution profits, but also ultimately added to the consumers' burden. This will be discussed further below. Although there were many problems in the market for materials, the reform enabled rural enterprises to advance to a new stage in which there were more opportunities to buy raw materials.

Second, other important markets such as the money market, the technology market and the labour market started to develop. For example, the stock markets in Shanghai and Shenzhen began operation with the approval of the department concerned under the State Council. In 1991, a national issuance of more than 60 types of securities exceeded 200 billion yuan; some 60 cities opened markets for the transfer of state treasury bonds; and the country had more than 500 stock exchange networks (Niu Genying, 1991, pp.11-2-14). The country's labour service institutions in 1991 reached over 8,000, while technological development markets and business organs were around 20,000 (Niu Genying,

1991, pp.11-2-14). In sum, the market developed very rapidly in a variety of sectors.

The expansion of the market created an environment favourable for the development of rural enterprises. In both developed and undeveloped areas alike, the main channels of purchase and sales for rural enterprises were markets, including direct procurement markets and cooperative markets among enterprises. According to a survey of rural industrial enterprises (Zhou Qiren and Hu Zhuangjun, 1989, p.116), the enterprises were themselves responsible for their purchase and marketing of 84.6 per cent of input goods and 90 per cent of product sales.

Du Haiyan (1990, pp.47-62) demonstrated that profits obtained from the assets in operation entirely hinged on the ability of township industrial enterprises to make use of market opportunities. Thus, rural enterprises had placed strategic emphasis on sales as well as purchases. This had led to a widely held belief that the success of rural enterprises had owed much to their marketing.

Rural enterprises' production and business activity were also affected substantially by the market situation. According to the surveys (Du Haiyan, 1988, pp.21-32), more than half of the sampled enterprises said that their production activities were primarily dependent upon the market. For example, in terms of enterprise fixed price regulations, market supply and demand factors had a major position in the way in which rural enterprises set prices. According to the surveys (Du Haiyan, 1988, pp.21-32), market supply and demand directly determined the way in which rural enterprises set prices although rural enterprises' prices were affected by state plans.

In short, from 1978 to 1992, the market had considerably developed, and a variety of markets have been established in China. The expansion of the market and establishment of different markets had created a favourable environment for the development of rural enterprises.

Some characteristics of the use of the market by rural enterprises

Rural enterprises had gradually developed some unique characteristics in the use of the market. William A. Byrd and N. Zhu (1990, pp.92-96) demonstrated that rural enterprises simultaneously used price competition and non-price competition. Price competition was an important ingredient in rural enterprises' market behaviour. In a situation of severe market competition, enterprises faced the problem of the jacking up of prices in the procurement of their raw and processed materials, and competition to lower prices in the marketing of their products.

Non-price competition had an even more important position in rural enterprise competitiveness. There had been the different patterns of competition: imitative competition, investment competition, innovative competition (William A. Byrd and N.Zhu, 1990, pp.92-96). Imitative competition was that a resourceful entrepreneur found a new product or process that had been successful elsewhere and earned high profits, and many imitators soon followed since entry was easy. Consequently prices and profits declined. Investment competition was similar to imitative competition. However, it involved large investments of community resources to build facilities that were capital intensive, and often use advanced, sometime even imported technology. Innovative competition was when some rural enterprises adopted innovation, which continually disrupted market equilibriums and led to improvements in products and efficiency.

In addition, as Du Haiyan (1990, pp.54-55) demonstrated, rural enterprises had used several methods for marketing. First, permanent, part-time and temporary marketing staff with the different payments were employed by rural enterprises. Second, marketing staff generally earned higher salary than other employees, and could also use operational fees to gain access to supply and sales links. Finally, rural enterprises also used agricultural and sideline products as quasi-currency to buy raw materials and sell their substandard but high priced goods to state commercial departments. Rural enterprises could also obtain part of state enterprises' profit by such means as giving sales commissions, paying sales agents, and making out blank invoices.

As the growth of rural enterprises expanded, competition became increasingly intense. According to studies conducted by the State Council's Rural Policy Research Center (Tu Xinjun, 1987, p.10), 48 per cent of the sample enterprises had competitors in their own township. Sample enterprises frequently cited 'society's limited supply capability', and 'too many enterprises need the same kinds of raw materials and energy resources'. They also blamed poor sales on 'overproduction of the same kinds of production'. The studies show that, based on sample enterprises, the value of output per hundred yuan of fixed assets rose from 291 yuan in 1981 to 320 yuan in 1985, but actual pretax profit fell in every year, from 64.5 yuan in 1981 to 47.5 yuan in 1985 (Tu Xinjun, 1987, p.10).

In short, rural enterprises' production and business activity were determined substantially by the market situation. There was the simultaneous existence of price competition and non-price competition in rural enterprise competitiveness; both were important, but the later was more critical for rural enterprises.

Conclusion

From 1978 to 1990, reform of the market had an important impact on the development of rural enterprises. Although China's free market system had not been completely established, the development of the market had been extremely helpful in boosting rural enterprises. Rural enterprises, free from state plan restrictions, had been able to buy much needed raw materials and equipment on the market and get financial assistance from society and individuals. As Du Haiyan (1988, p.60) pointed out, 'changes in the macroeconomic environment and in market conditions created space for the survival and expansion of TVP (township, village and private) industry'.

Therefore, reform of the market had been very important in relation to the development of rural enterprises. As I have discussed in Chapter Two, from late 1988 to 1991, the central planners have prevailed, rural enterprises were a major target of this retrenchment policy, and rural enterprises faced a considerable shortage of materials and funds. At least two-thirds of the enterprises were affected, causing enormous losses to local interests and huge rural unemployment. The reporter for *TE* Journal wrote: 'it finds that the non-state businesses grow bigger and stronger still, making the next clampdown in favour of state firms that much harder to impose and maintain' (*TE*, 1 June 1991). Despite the national retrenchment policy, rural enterprises had managed to survive and even expand.

However, the expansion of rural enterprises' markets, however, had faced serious challenges from both urban enterprises and local protectionism. China's urban enterprises had undergone structural changes, and their production had been less dictated by mandatory plans. Urban enterprises and rural enterprises had competed under the most unfair terms; urban enterprises unlike rural enterprises had huge capital, advanced technologies, and well-trained personnel; they were well supplied with raw materials under state plans, and had well-established sales channels and good information networks; more important, large industries enjoyed economies of scale beyond the reach of rural enterprises.

In addition, rural enterprises had also faced serious local protectionism. This had restrained further expansion of rural enterprises's markets. During the late 1980s, some local leaders tried to safeguard their local interests by creating barriers and checkpoints to prevent goods leaving their territory, with some provinces even employing armed police forces and militia units at provincial borders (Shuan Breslin, 1995). Other provinces adopted more sophisticated protectionist methods. They used the central government austerity policies and its programmes for strengthening market management, and rectifying wholesale commerce and control sales of fake and inferior products as pretexts for excluding goods from outside the region. Some provinces even imposed fixed ratios on the sale of goods by commercial departments, wholesale trades and retail stores (Robert Delfs, 1990, p.89). As a result, local protectionism had restrained the development of rural enterprises.

From 1978 to 1992, the government had changed rural employment strategies and regional development strategies. The changes of these strategies had important implications on the development of rural enterprises. In the next chapter, I shall examine how the changes of these strategies had influenced the development of rural enterprises.

5 Implications of rural employment and regional development strategies for rural enterprises

In the previous chapter, I have discussed how market reform and market expansion influenced the development of rural enterprises. In this chapter, I shall discuss the implications of rural employment and regional development strategies for rural enterprises.

Government strategies for rural employment and their implications for rural enterprises

From 1978 to 1992, the success of the rural reforms and China's insufficient amount of cultivated land compared with the size of its labour force, had resulted in large numbers of rural surplus labour. The majority of rural surplus labour force could not move to the cities since the cities had yet to find a way to solve their own unemployment problems. The government sought to deal with the problem locally rather than permitting thousands of people to swarm into the cities. The main strategy was to encourage peasants to set up rural enterprises through self-accumulated capital and bank loans. Rural enterprises had played a very important role in solving the problem of rural surplus labour. In this section, I shall concentrate on the Chinese government's measures for rural surplus labour and employment in rural enterprises rather than discuss the general issues of rural employment. In doing so, I shall first briefly assess the extent of unemployment in rural areas. Secondly, I shall examine the government's strategies for solving rural unemployment. Thirdly, I shall consider the relation between the development of small towns and rural employment. Finally, I shall discuss the employment in rural enterprises.

Unemployment in rural areas

China is the most highly populated country in the world. The population density per square kilometre of the 30 provinces, autonomous regions and municipalities on the mainland, was 118 persons in 1990 (*BR*, 17-23 December 1990, p.22). Moreover, the majority of Chinese people were still engaged in agriculture.

Since 1949, urban migration in China had been controlled. As Taylor noted, 'Administrative measures, such as the household registration system and the urban grain ration system have traditionally served as barriers to the spontaneous migration of peasants to large cities' (Taylor, 1988, p.745). As a result, China's farmers had been forced to stay in rural areas to make a living. Taylor argued that 'The primary reason why rural surplus labour has continued to exit in China is that tight constraints on rural to urban migration and the existence of fixed land resources in rural areas have forced many more Chinese farmers to make a living from tilling the soil than is necessary' (Taylor, 1988, p.745).

It is difficulty to measure exactly how many surplus labourers there were in China's rural areas. The different findings by the different analysts indicated the same conclusion: more than 100 million were redundant and about 30 per cent of China's rural work force was in surplus (cf. Taylor, 1988, pp.749-753). In 1991, it was estimated that along the coast migrant numbering about 23 million to 80 million were looking for work (*TE*, 22 June 1991). One southern city, Guangzhou, attracted a floating population estimated at 516,000. The situation became so severe that the officials issued an 'urgent circular' for 'the greatest efforts possible to keep them from leaving home' (*TE*, 22 June 1991).

Therefore, if the Chinese government could not provide enough jobs for its rural surplus labour, China's social and economic development would be seriously disrupted. Solving rural surplus labour became a very important issue.

Strategies for rural employment

Jeffrey R. Taylor's research (1988, pp.739-744) indicated that the Chinese government adopted on the following strategies for improving rural labour utilization from 1949 to 1978.

The first strategy was to raise the labour intensity of farming by promoting multiple cropping, intercropping, deep ploughing, extensive fertilization, and expanded irrigation. Taylor demonstrated that average annual labour expended per hectare increased sharply from 1953 to 1978.

The second strategy was to organize the construction of irrigation canals, dams, roads and other forms of rural infrastructure to reduce unemployment. In particular, during the winter months, rural construction campaigns increased labour utilization.

The final strategy was to develop urban industry to recruit rural labour. There were considerable numbers of peasants recruited into urban industry during the Great Leap Forward and during the Cultural Revolution, when urban youths were sent to rural areas.

However, the development of rural enterprises did not become an important strategy for rural employment before 1978, and was only considered as a supplement to agricultural development rather than as a strategic measure to increase rural employment.

Since 1978 when the production responsibility system was introduced, rural surplus labour had become visible as a serious social problem. A number of scholars discussed possible ways to deal with this problem (cf. Li Shihui, 1987, pp.49-53, Li Qingzeng, 1986, pp.8-11, Feng Lanrui and Jiang Weiyu, 1988, pp.64-77). Three main strategies can be identified: (1) leaving the land and the native place, (2) not leaving the land, nor the native place, (3) leaving the native place but not the land.

Leaving the land and the native place meant that rural labourers entered the cities. The income differential between urban inhabitants and peasants provided a strong incentive for farmers, especially young people, to flow into the cities. Since 1978, a considerable number of peasants had gone to the cities to work as maids, housekeepers and tailors, and to open restaurants. Some peasants entered urban factories and were officially employed, but most were accepted as contract workers and casual labourers. However, as Feng Lanrui and Jiang Weiyu (1988, pp.64-77) argued, the cities' accommodation capacity for rural labourers was restricted by the number of jobs available in the cities. In addition, the unchecked entry of peasants into the cities was bound to cause difficulties in the areas of housing, transportation, health care and administration. Some Chinese scholars proposed that the Chinese government should encourage the peasants to enter the cities and open factories to develop medium scale cities to large scale. However, as Feng Lanrui and Jiang Weiyu (1988, pp.64-77) pointed out, this proposal was still at the stage of theoretical study and policy exploration and had not become a reality.

Not leaving the land, nor the native place had two elements: first it referred to the adjustment of the internal structure of crop farming. On the one hand, this strategy would reduce the acreage sown to grain crops and labour input. On the other hand, it would expand the acreage for labour intensive economic crops and labor input. Second, it referred to the development of peasants' part-time production. When peasants were in slack seasons, they engaged in diversified undertakings, including industrial, commercial, transport, labour and other service businesses and various kinds of household sideline production. However, in this strategy, there was the limitation of adjustment of the production set-up within the framework of farming because of the inadequate scientific and technological knowledge, the decrease of land, and the increase of population (Feng Lanrui and Jiang Weiyu, 1988, pp.64-77).

Leaving the land but not the native place meant peasants set up rural enterprises locally. This can include peasants engaging in rural enterprises full-time or part-time. After 1978, peasants had been allowed to engage in non-farming activities. They undertook industrial, commercial, building, transport and service business near their small towns or their villages but they did not change their permanent residence registration nor their grain ration relations. Their families still stayed in the countryside.

Many articles in Chinese journals were published to support the third strategy. However, some Chinese scholars (cf. Li Shihui, 1987, pp.49-53) held that China should not depend on the small towns solely to absorb the rural surplus labour force in their localities, when the rural population still accounted for 80 per cent of China's total population. They pointed out that the density of population in the cities, not including the 16 major cities such as Shanghai and Beijing, was not high. It was totally possible for these cities to provide employment for rural surplus labour.

Feng Lanrui and Jiang Weiyu (1988, pp.64-77) also argued that while it was true that most rural enterprises were located in areas near and closely related to large and medium-sized cities and coastal areas, in the areas far from big cities the conditions for agricultural production were poor, and peasants even had problems of obtaining adequate food and clothing. It was impossible for them to set up rural enterprises to solve the problem of rural surplus labour.

Nevertheless, although the strategy of leaving the land but not the native place had some limitations, the Chinese government had adopted this strategy from 1978 to 1992. On the one hand, the migration from rural areas to urban areas had been controlled. On the other hand, the construction and development of small towns utilizing a large number of rural surplus labourers had been undertaken to prevent their migration into big cities. Over the years, millions of peasants had left the land, but not the village, to enter rural enterprises. Their practice had become a strategic principle formulated by the Chinese government from 1978 to 1992. One official document clearly indicated this strategic principle:

> It is estimated that by the end of this century China's countryside will have 450 million (labour force). By then, crop cultivation will be able to employ only 30 per cent of the labour force, and forestry, animal husbandry and fishery, just 20 per cent. Another 10 per cent can find employment in the cities, leaving 40 per cent looking for work in other directions. They will mainly be employed in industry, construction, transportation and communications, commercial undertakings and other service trades in the rural towns as well as the family-operated industrial and sideline occupations in the rural areas (towns included), otherwise they will become a serious social problem (The Minister of Agriculture, Animal Husbandry and Fishery and the Ministry's Leading Party Group. (1984), *SWB/FE* 26 March).

Thus, the development of rural enterprises represented an important strategy of solving the employment problem in China.

The development of small towns

From 1978 to 1992, China's government had maintained tight control to prevent peasants migrating to big cities, but it had taken a more liberal policy in allowing peasants to work in small towns. The small town boom had provided job opportunities for millions of peasants in industrial production, commercial activities and various kinds of service trades.

Many Chinese scholars supported the development of small towns. The main arguments were as follows: small towns could link the urban market to the rural market since small towns could serve as distribution centres for agricultural and sideline products as well as industrial goods. Small towns could become processing centres for agricultural and sideline products and play a supporting role for urban industries. Furthermore, small towns could enrich the cultural life of peasants, and change the overall relationship between cities and the countryside and develop the rural economy. Finally the policy served to narrow the gap between town and country. The assumption was that China's cities were already fully expanded and their factories and population had reached saturation point. The growth rate of population in middle-sized cities could basically meet the needs of their own development. So the many small towns in China, which had plenty of room for development and could hold many people, were targeted for expansion. The surplus labour in the rural areas should be encouraged to work in small towns nearby their homes. This could help the big and middle-sized cities reduce the pressure of increasing population and avoid the 'city disease' caused by the expansion of population.

Fei Xiaotong, a renowned Chinese sociologist, strongly supported the development of rural enterprises in China (Fei Xiaotong, 1985a, pp.24-26). He pointed out that during the process of industrialization in capitalist countries, many peasants in the countryside were on the brink of bankruptcy. The farmers were forced to leave, and swarmed into the cities. Industrialization in China was, however, following an utterly different road from that of capitalist countries. On the basis of a prospering agricultural sector, it could run collectively owned township industries. These industries, by assisting, consolidating and promoting the agricultural economy, brought about the simultaneous development of agriculture, sideline occupations and industry.

As Taylor (1988, pp.758-761) also argued, China has faced rising food requirements with an agricultural work force that was increasingly composed of the elderly, women and children, and those with relatively low educational levels. To counter this trend, China's governments had strongly encouraged part-time farming, rather than a complete migration from the land for rural-to-urban migrants. In addition, since rural unemployment in China had traditionally been seasonal, peasants had long been encouraged to do jobs in small towns, but return home to help farming when labour was short of supply in the busy planting and harvesting seasons.

Thus, the Chinese government's policy was to actively encourage peasants to move to small towns located near farmers' plots rather than to large and medium-sized cities. For example, in April 1983 the promulgation of the State Council's 'Regulations Concerning Co-operative Endeavours of City and Town Labourers' allowed peasants to work in market towns while retaining their rural household registrations (Hu Yinkang, 1985, p.37). A further loosening of constraints on rural-to-small town migration took place when the State Council released its 'Circular On Questions Regarding the Settlement of Peasants Entering Towns' in October 1984 (*XHYB*, No.10, 1984, p.102). This regulation was popular although residents of these towns had to obtain their own food, and could not rely on urban grain reserves (Taylor 1988, p.759). This meant that voluntary migration to small towns was permissible under the condition that grain was provided by themselves. During the eighth plenary session of the 13th CCP Central Committee on 29th November 1991, the Central Committee called for the development of secondary and tertiary industries, the stepping up of the development of small rural industrial districts and market towns, and the opening up of more avenues for rural labour force transfer (*SWB/FE*, 3 January 1992). It seems clear that the development of rural enterprises was the single most important government strategy for utilising rural surplus labour.

With the encouragement of China's state policy, the small towns had mushroomed. There were about 8,000 medium sized and small towns across the country, in addition to 50,000 rural market towns in 1986 (Lei Xilu, 1986). Small towns included towns, county seats and factory and mining districts and commercial centres. Towns were administrative divisions ratified by the provinces, municipalities and autonomous regions according to State Council's regulations. They were equivalent to townships under the county governments. Generally, each county had a county seat. Most of the county seats had city or township governments. In 1982, there were 2,800 county seats (*BR*, 21 May 1984). Factory and mining districts referred to those industrial and residential areas independent of nearby cities and towns. They did not have city or township governments. There were 54,000 commercial centres, most of which were also the seats of township governments (the people's communes in the past), and they still had the foundations for light industry, handicrafts, commerce and services (*BR*, 21 May 1984).

Small towns had the characteristics of both the cities and the countryside, and of industry and agriculture. Some of them had been gradually developed into new kinds of medium sized and small cities. The growth of small towns had changed the relationship between cities and the countryside and had enabled rural enterprises to concentrate in small towns. Small towns had been built into comprehensive economic, technical and cultural centres for the development of agriculture, industry, commerce and transportation services in which rural energy resources could be put to more rational use.

Small towns helped absorb the surplus labour force and checked the flow of peasants into large and medium sized cities, by providing job opportunities for millions of peasants in industrial, commercial activities and various kinds of service trades. It was estimated that by the end of this century China's rural towns will provide jobs for 300 million people no longer needed on the farms, a figure amounting to 40 per cent of the total rural population (Wang Dacheng, 1985).

In summary, the Chinese government's policy of encouraging the development of small towns had stimulated a boom for small towns and created favourable conditions for production and investment for rural enterprises. As a result, the development of small towns in China had created immensely more employment for peasants.

Employment in rural enterprises

The development of rural enterprises had played a very important role in absorbing rural surplus labour. In 1989 township enterprises employed 95.4 million people in the countryside, making up 23.8 per cent of the country's labour force (Wu Yunhe, 1989b). As Taylor (1988, p.756) indicated, agricultural employment in rural areas grew at an annual average rate of less than one per cent between 1978 and 1986, whereas rural non-agricultural employment had quadrupled in the short span of nine years.

However, the development of rural enterprises of opportunity and ability had been extremely uneven because of both comparative economic advantage and China's regional development strategy. As a result, the imbalance in the development of rural enterprises had made an important impact on spatial distribution of rural employment. Employment in rural enterprises was highly concentrated in the coastal provinces and the municipalities of Beijing, Tianjin, and Shanghai. I shall analyze this issue later.

The majority of workers in rural enterprises were engaged in industrial activities. The rest were engaged in agriculture, construction, transport, commerce, catering and the service trade. The information (The State Statistical Bureau, PRC, 1988, p.288) shows that 60-70 per cent of workers in rural enterprises were engaged in industrial activities from 1978 to 1987. As the different branches of rural industries are analyzed, a large proportion of employment in both townships and villages run industries involved in manufactured goods of building materials and other non-metal minerals, garments, yarn and farm equipment (The State Statistical Bureau, PRC, 1988, p.288). Rural industries not only accounted for a large proportion of employment in rural enterprises but also played a very important role in China's national economy. For example, in 1990 rural industries supplied almost one-third of China's coal, cement, paper and silk products, and 60-80 per cent of the country's garments, yarn and farm equipment (*SWB/FE/W*, 25 September 1991).

The numbers of labourers in secondary industries, including food processing, sideline production, small mines, manufacturing and building, reached nearly 39 million in 1985, 73.7 per cent more than in 1980. Finally tertiary industry, involving transport, commerce and service businesses, employed more than 28.4 million workers, 135 per cent more than in 1980 (Lei Xilu, 1986). Nevertheless, rural industrial employment had grown at a somewhat slower rate than other sectors of rural enterprises. The reason was that peasants had shown more interest in investing their funds in housing. This had created vast opportunities for individuals transporting the materials and supplies that these sectors needed.

The majority of employees in rural enterprises were from rural areas. A survey in 1987 (Han Baocheng, 1987) shows that 88 per cent of employees in these enterprises were rural people, the rest urban. Each of these worker families had an average of 2.82 able-bodied men, with 1.64 persons working in rural enterprises and making 63.6 per cent of the family's total income. As many as 91 per cent of these households still had contracted fields which supplied them with their grain needs and 71 per cent of enterprise employees took part in farming during the busy seasons (Han Baocheng, 1987). This indicates that workers in rural enterprises still had a close relation with agriculture.

However, the rate of increase in employment in rural enterprises had slowed down in late 1980s. He Kang, chairman of the China Township Enterprise Association, disclosed (Sun Jian, 1991, p.1) that in the first five years of 1980s the increase of employment in rural enterprises was 44 million and in the last five years 22 million, so in the former the annual average was 8 million and in the latter the annual average was 4 million.

From late 1988 to 1991, the Chinese leadership implemented a retrenchment policy. In the countryside many rural enterprises had been forced to close down. The retrenchment policy increased the local burden of rural surplus labour. Since rural enterprises were the major way of easing the problem of too many people tilling a fixed area of land, soon after this road was obstructed, albeit temporarily, large-scale bankruptcy of rural enterprises occurred and squeezed large numbers of peasant-workers out of employment. The information indicated that township enterprises absorbed 50 per cent less rural workers in 1989 than 1988 (*JPRS*-CAR-90-055 26 July 1990, p.58), and about 3 million rural enterprises were closed down in 1989 (*SWB/FE/W*, 5 September 1990, Xinhua, 27 August 1990). Especially in the construction sector many former peasants had been fired and sent back to the countryside. For example, Shanghai cut its contingent of construction workers by 100,000 or one-seventh in 1989 in an attempt to curb excessive capital construction (*SWB/FE/W*, 3 January 1990, Xinhua 15 December 1989).

Moreover, during this period, some conservative leaders did not want the development of rural enterprises to threaten the dominance of state enterprises in the national economy, and tried to control the development of rural enterprises. They planned that during 1990s only about 3 million persons will be assimilated every year, so the total will be 120 million persons by the year 2,000 (Sun Jian, 1991, p.1). However, according to the preliminary plan, the total output value of township enterprises should double by 1990 over 1985, and then would have a two-third increase by the year 2,000. About 170 million labourers would be employed (Lei Xilu, 1986).

Although China's leadership preferred to develop state enterprises rather than rural enterprises, state enterprises could not provide sufficient opportunities for employment. Since the Chinese government can not afford the social risk of disturbance, it will still have to depend on further development of rural enterprise to solve the problem of rural surplus labour.

Implications of regional development strategies for rural enterprises

In this section, I shall discuss the impact of China's regional development policies for development imbalances of rural enterprises. In doing so, first, I shall examine regional development imbalances of rural enterprises, then I shall analyze the impacts of China's regional development policy for regional development imbalances of rural enterprises.

Regional development imbalances of rural enterprises

China can be divided into three regions: the coastal developed region, the central region, the interior backward region. The coastal developed region includes the nine provinces and municipalities of Shanghai, Tianjin, Beijing, Jiangsu, Zhejiang, Liaoning, Shandong, Guangdong and Hebei. The central region includes the eleven provinces of Shanxi, Fujian, Jilin, Hubei, Hunan Heilongjiang, Henan, Anhui, Shaanxi, Jiangxi and Sichuan. The western backward region includes the ten provinces and autonomous regions of Ningxia, Gansu, Neimenggu, Guangxi, Xinjiang, Hainan, Yunnan, Guizhou, Qinghai and Xizang.

Ke Bingsheng used two indexes to analyze regional development of rural industry in 1988: the value of the rural industry output per capita of agricultural population (value of output of rural industry/ rural population), and geographical density (value of output of a region's rural industry/territorial area of the region). The coastal region's value of the rural industry output per capita of agricultural population was 5.2 times that the central region and 14.2 times that of the western region. The geographical density of the coastal region's value of rural industry output was 8.5 times that of the central region and 167 times that of western region. Over 80 percent of China's gross rural industry exports were made by the nine provinces and the cities of the coast in 1988 (Ke Bingsheng, 1990, pp.33-36).

In term of absolute values, in 1982 the value of rural industry output per capita of agricultural population in the coastal region was 109 yuan/person higher than the central region and 138 yuan/person higher than the western region; in 1988 the difference between the two had increased sharply to 2,140 yuan/person and 3,191 yuan/person, respectively, a more than 20 fold increase (Ke Bingsheng, 1990, pp 33-36).

Li Shih Chun's study (1987, p.33) also shows that regional development imbalances had become very wide. In 1986 the gross value of output from rural enterprises in 8 provinces and cities, Beijing, Tianjin, Shanghai, Liaoning, Shandong, Jiangsu, Zhejiang, Guangdong, accounted for 50 per cent of the gross value of output for rural enterprises nationwide. By contrast, the gross value of output from rural enterprises in 8 northwestern and southwestern provinces, Shaanxi, Gansu, Ningxia, Qinghai, Xinjiang, Guangxi, Guizhou, and Yunnan, accounted for only 5 percent of the gross value of output for rural enterprises nationwide (Li Shih-chun, 1987, p.33). Furthermore, regional development imbalances had also appeared in different regions of a single province. For example, the gross value of output from rural enterprises in Suzhou, Wuxi, and Changzhou three southern Jiangsu cities near Shanghai accounted for 50 per cent of gross value of output for the entire Jiangsu Province in 1986. By contrast, rural enterprises in Xuzhou, Huaiyin, Yancheng, and Lianyun -- four cities in northern Jiangsu accounted for only 11 per cent (Li Shihchun, 1987, p.33).

The unbalanced development of rural enterprises had widened the regional income differential since farmers' income from rural enterprises had become the main source for farmers' income increase. For example, between 1982 and 1988 income supplied by the rural industry of developed coastal provinces and cities to each person in the rural areas increased from 27 yuan to 200 yuan, while that of the central and western undeveloped region increased from only 2-5 yuan to 9-27 yuan (Ke Bingsheng, 1990, pp 33-36). Thus, the gap between China's east and west in terms of production and living standards in rural areas had widened.

Implications of regional development strategies for rural enterprises

Yang Dali (1990, pp.230-257) demonstrated that there had been a significant change of China's regional development strategy since 1978. From 1953 to 1978, China's regional development strategy emphasized regional industrial balance and sought to correct the inherited coast-interior imbalance by directing a large portion of industrial investment into inland areas. Since 1978 China's leaders adopted the 'uneven development strategy', which focused on economic results, and emphasized regional comparative advantage, accepted regional disparities as inevitable, encouraged foreign investment and international interaction, and fostered technological innovation. China's government had increased investment of fixed assets in coastal areas since the late 1970s. In addition, the favourable policies were granted to the coastal region, enabling it to attract most of foreign investment. In addition, the favourable policies were granted to coastal areas and especially the Special Economic Zones. As a result, rural enterprises in the coastal region enjoyed vast advantages in their dealing with other provinces and they had more business opportunities to cooperate with state enterprises and foreign enterprises.

Since 1978, China's government had given some preferential financial treatments and tax relief for rural enterprises in poor areas so that these policies could bring these areas out of poverty. However, as Yang Dali (1990, pp.255-256) demonstrated, the centre's policy towards the poor areas had been undermined by three factors: first, government and party administrative expenditures were higher in poor areas than in more developed areas. These poor areas had less funds left for the development. Secondly, bank deposits in the poor areas preferred to invest in the more developed central and coastal regions since the intervention by multi-tier, low quality, and overstaffed governments and a host of geographical, cultural and social factors reduced returns on investments and frightened potential investors away. Finally, poorer conditions in the underdeveloped area had made it difficult to attract and keep talented personnel, thereby making development even more difficulties. Thus, although China's government had implemented some policies to develop rural enterprises in the poor areas in the 1980s, the Chinese government's ability to alleviate regional development imbalances of rural enterprises was limited.

The uneven development of the economy and comparative advantages were another reason for development imbalances of rural enterprises. S. Breslin (1995) demonstrated that uneven development and comparative advantage not only existed between provinces, but also within provincial boundaries. In particular, municipalities with high economic status had massive comparative advantages over the rest of their provinces.

The coastal regions had enjoyed superior factor endowments compared with the interior. Coastal regions possessed an industrial labour force with long years of experience, and also accumulated superior managerial skills compared with the interior. Coastal areas such as Jiangsu, Zhejiang, and other economically developed areas had more technological personnel than interior areas. Hence, coastal regions could also provide more assistance for rural enterprises in terms of technological personnel. The fundamental economic advantage of poorer, more backward areas was their low wage rates. However, capital and entrepreneurs were largely immobile and were not attracted to poor areas. As a result, the advantage of low wage rates in the interior was of limited use.

In addition, the development of rural enterprises was contingent upon the availability of urban markets. A developed urban economy could provide its surrounding rural area with vast quantities of timely economic information, which in turn stimulates growth of the rural market economy. A developed urban economy with substantial demand for products from rural enterprises undoubtedly stimulated growth of rural enterprises.

As the income gap between coast and interior regions became worse, China's government soon realized that the growing income gap was to a large extent due to the regional development imbalances of rural enterprises, and has promulgated special policy for the development of rural enterprises in central and western regions since 1992. In June 1992, the Ministry of Agriculture convened a symposium on strategies for rural enterprise development in central regions in the old revolutionary base Jinggangshan, Jiangxi Province. In November 1992, a national conference to exchange experiences in rural enterprise development in central and western regions was held in Xian City (*ZGXZQYB*, 22 September 1994). The State Council's draft, 'Decision on Speeding up the Development of Rural Enterprises in Central and Western Regions', was discussed in this conference, and was formally issued in February 1993 (*ZGXZQYB*, 22 September 1994). The People's Bank of China also planned in November 1992 to increase five billion yuan annually from 1993 to 2000 to support the development of rural enterprises in central and western regions (*ZGXZQYB*, 22 September 1994). Thus, China's government has begun to pay more attention to the development of rural enterprises in central and western regions since 1992.

The information (*ZGXZQYB*, 24 May 1995) shows that since China's government implemented special policies on speeding up the development of rural enterprises in the central and western regions, rural enterprises in the central and western regions indeed increased more rapidly than in the coastal region.

Summary

From 1978 to 1992, regional development imbalances of rural enterprises had widened. Rural enterprises were highly concentrated in the coastal provinces and the municipalities of Beijing, Tianjin, and Shanghai, but very undeveloped in the broad interior regions of central plain and western China. The development imbalances of rural enterprises had also widened regional income differentials. China's regional development strategy and comparative advantages in coastal areas were the main reasons for regional development imbalances of rural enterprises. China's government has began to formulate special policy to develop rural enterprises in central and western regions since 1992.

Conclusion

The government had been incapable of solving the problem of rural surplus labour, and was forced to let localities deal with the problem of rural unemployment. The urbanization which accompanied industrialization created problems for most developing countries: millions of impoverished farmers had crowded cities beyond capacity. The development of China's rural enterprises however provided an exception. The growth of rural enterprises had provided a local solution to the problem of rural surplus labour. China's experience had shown that in shifting rural surplus labour toward the development of rural enterprises, not only had this avoided large-scale shifts in rural population, but it had also avoided a decline and dissolution of the countryside.

In the future, the transformation of rural surplus labour will still concentrate on small towns. As I have discussed above, the development of small towns has many social and economic advantages. 'China has decided to check the expansion of cities with over half million people. Cities with fewer than 500,000 people will be developed rationally and the development of small towns with less than 200,000 residents will be encouraged' (Lei Xilu, 1986). In particular, the focus will still be placed on the development of county seats and small towns within county boundaries. At the same time, rural enterprises would be encouraged to gather at small towns. However, the main factor restricting the movement of rural population to small towns is the current land system, which serves as a guarantee of peasants' production as well as a guarantee of social security. It will be necessary that a pension system will be introduced in rural enterprises and together with new social security mechanisms, this will replace the social security presently provided by the land.

It is essential for China's government to take further measures to reduce the regional development imbalances of rural enterprises. Wang Tuoyu (1990, pp.270-273) provided some suggestions for reducing regional development

78

imbalances of rural enterprises: free interregional flow of labour and of other factors of production should be encouraged; private enterprises should be allowed to develop further; and limited amount of state support available for the more backward areas should be targeted at sound investment projects and at areas with low per capita incomes and poorer agricultural resources. China's government has also paid more attention to develop rural enterprises in central and western regions since 1992. As a result, rural enterprises in the central and western regions have increased rapidly in last few years.

From 1978 to 1992, the government had provided more preferential financial and taxation policies for rural enterprises. Thus, in the next chapter, I shall discuss China's government financial and taxation policies for rural enterprises.

6 Financial and taxation policies towards rural enterprises

In Chapter Five, I have discussed the implications of China's government rural employment strategies and regional development strategies for rural enterprises. In this chapter, I shall examine the government financial and taxation policies towards rural enterprises. I shall analyze these policies under the following headings. First I shall examine the state's financial policy towards rural enterprises and its implications. Secondly I shall discuss the state's tax policy towards rural enterprises. Thirdly I shall consider the sources of capital in rural enterprises. Finally I shall examine the fundraising for rural enterprises.

Financial policy towards rural enterprises

It was estimated that 80 per cent of rural enterprises depended to a greater or lesser extent on bank loans. Roughly 20 per cent of rural enterprises depended entirely on bank loans to run their businesses. Among the entire nation's rural enterprises, operating fund loans accounted for approximately 50 per cent of total operating funds, and for an even higher percentage of fixed capital (Nan Bei, 1989, p.3). Therefore, financial policy towards rural enterprises was a very important factor which determined the extent of the development of rural enterprises.

From 1978 to 1992, the policy of granting credit to rural enterprises had been more liberal than before, but credit fund supply had been changeable. The information (*NYJJWT*, No.23, October 1991, pp.20-25) shows that growth of credit supply fluctuated greatly during the period 1980 to 1990. Fluctuations in aggregate credit occurred during three periods: From 1979 to 1984, following several years of rural enterprises readjustment, rural enterprises moved from an early development stage to a stage of rapid development. Credit was tightened from 1981 to the end of 1983, but eased in 1984. During this period, credit issuance peaked twice, the highest peak took place in 1984 when credit increased 108 per cent over that of 1983.

The Communist Party Central Committee's document no 1 for 1985 set out ten measures aimed at encouraging a market-oriented rural economy. This document further called for relaxing rural financial policies, raising returns on funds, and encouraging rural credit and insurance business. Local credit cooperatives were allowed to operate independently. The document said that the money they raised would be put at their disposal after they delivered a set amount of reserve funds to the Agricultural Bank of China. The term of loan repayment for equipment purchase was one to five years while for technological transformation of old enterprises, the repayment term was one to three years, and for overhauling of equipment, it was one year. The interest rate on loans was also reduced. The document stated that planning, supply, financial, banking and communications departments at all levels of government should let the township and village enterprises open accounts and give them guidance and support. Thus, credit supply rose greatly in 1986 and 1987.

In the fourth quarter of 1987, however, the State Council handed down instructions to tighten finance and credit in an effort to stabilize currency and product prices, and therefore credit supply was tightened again. This contradiction in central government policy had not been the only occasion since 1978 when later pronouncements and decrees had conflicted with earlier statements. For enterprise managers trying to adapt to the rigours and demands of a newly emerging market economy, such fluctuations in government policy made the process of planning (even in the short term) extremely difficult.

From late 1988 to 1991, Chinese conservative leadership dominated in China. Credit supply had shown a downward trend. In 1989, the increase in credit reached the lowest. Rural enterprises thus faced serious financial difficulty. The information shows that if the growth rate in 1989 for rural enterprises was assumed to be 15 per cent, that would demand at least 25 million yuan in operating funds. The state in practice only satisfied a small part of that sum (Nan Bei, 1989).

The retrenchment policy had particularly hit the expansion of newly opened enterprises. Many of the newly opened enterprises had to rely on bank credit for working capital. Retrenchment policy had caused a considerable proportion of enterprise assets to be left idle. For example, Xinxing Building Materials Plant in Luhe County, Jiangsu, with the help of county townships, had received a loan of 11.5 million yuan to import advanced Italian equipment for the manufacture of various types of newly developed building tiles. In October 1988, the equipment was installed and put into operation. Because of the shortage of funds, materials, and electrical power, in 1989, the three production lines having an annual production capacity of 7.5 million square meters were only able to produce 20-30 thousand square meters. They had not even begun to pay off the interest on their loan itself. A large plant and advanced equipment were idle, therefore creating a vast amount of waste (Yu Guoyao and Li Yandong, 1989, pp.22-27).

The fluctuation in the total credit supply had been attributed to the following political and economic factors. First, as I have demonstrated in Chapter two and Chapter Three, rural enterprise policies had been inconsistent because of the struggle of conservatives and reformists within China's leadership. Some conservative leaders emphasized the development of state enterprises and adopted a policy to definitely incline state enterprises to acquire credit supply, energy and raw materials. In particular, when economic development overheated and market supply became tight, restriction of bank credit towards rural enterprises was imposed. Second, as Wang Xingchun (*NYJJWT*, No.23, October 1991, pp.20-25) demonstrated, credit supply was directly influenced by the agricultural harvest. In good harvest years, rural enterprises had a solid base and developed very rapidly. As soon as a lean harvest occurred, credit supply was directed to grain and cotton production. Third, China had only undertaken partial reform of the market. Market mechanisms for regulating and controlling the total volume of credit for rural enterprises had not fully been developed. The government mainly depended on the plan to control the supply of credit. Excessive control also resulted in large fluctuations of credit supply (*NYJJWT*, No.23, October 1991, pp.20-25).

The information (*NYJJWT*, No.23, October 1991, pp.20-25) shows that township and village enterprise credit as a percentage of all national credit increased 2.1 times between 1983 and 1990; however, during the same period, township and village gross output value as a percentage of total social gross output value increased 3.8 times, much faster than the change in the percentage of credit. In 1990, gross output value of township and village enterprise as a percentage of social gross output value reached 25 per cent, but township and village enterprise credit accounted for only 8.3 per cent of total national bank credit. Thus, rural enterprises had used relatively little credit input to produce a fairly large value output. This further indicates that the government had still adopted discriminating policy against rural enterprises. Thus, rural enterprises had to raise funds from individuals and society. An informal financial market had inevitably appeared to supply the fund requirements of rural enterprises. I shall further discuss this issue later in this chapter.

However, despite such disturbance from political and economic factors, financial policy towards rural enterprises was generally more liberal during 1980s than in any previous period. In addition, the government established special funds for supporting rural enterprises. There were two sources of such supporting funds. As one source, rural enterprises were allowed to take 1 per cent out of their after-tax profits to be used by the administrative departments for rural enterprises. The other source of funding was the assistance from the financial department allocated for developing rural enterprises. Such funds were distributed through consultations between the local financial departments at various levels and the administrative departments for rural enterprises. The supporting funds were not gratuitous. There was a deadline for using such funds, and when this time period expired, the return of the unused funds was demanded so that they could be used over again on a constant, revolving basis. Accounts of enterprise funds and financial assistance funds were required to be kept by the administrative departments for rural enterprises and by the financial departments concerned respectively (The Minister of Agriculture, Animal Husbandry and Fishery and the Ministry's Leading Party Group. (1984), *SWB/FE*, 26 March).

Loans for rural enterprises were mainly used as circulating capital, and as fixed capital formation, as repaying temporary loans and as meeting the higher prices of raw and semifinished materials, energy, etc. To take 1985 as an example (*NCJR*, No 24, 16 December 1986, p.1), the uses of loans were mainly as follows:

First, a very large portion of the loans was used as fixed capital. In 1985, the value of fixed assets of enterprises at the township and village levels in the country increased 17 billion yuan (*NCJR*, Beijing, No 24, 16 December 1986, p.1).

Second, a large amount of credit was used to help enterprises to repay temporary loans. In 1985, a policy was implemented to tighten credit for township enterprises throughout the country. The enterprises' sales increased 44 per cent, fixed assets increased 59 per cent, and self-generated circulating funds increased 53 per cent. Credit extended to them as circulating funds increased only 4.8 billion yuan, or 22 per cent. To keep production and business operations going, rural enterprises, particularly those operating on a regular basis, were forced to raise funds by delaying wage payments or defaulting on loans. In 1985, rural enterprises owed workers and staff members more than 2 billion yuan in back wages and defaulted on payments for goods totalling some 5 billion yuan. They had to borrow nearly 3 billion yuan from units and individuals. Most of these temporary loans were repaid out of their sales receipts normally used to buy raw and semifinished materials. According to typical case surveys and national accounting analysis, about 5 billion yuan, or 38 per cent, of the increased 1986 credit was used to repay the temporary loans raised by the enterprises in 1985 (*NCJR*, Beijing, No 24, 16 December 1986, p.1).

Third, more loans were extended owing to market factors. Bank loans increased to meet the higher prices of raw and semifinished materials, energy, etc. According to typical cases studied, about 20 per cent of the credit increase was caused by price rises. For example, the purchasing price of fresh tea leaves rose about 30 per cent, and the prices of feed and raw materials rose nearly 50 per cent. Owing to the state's strict control over the scale of investment in fixed assets and other reasons in 1985, the building materials, machinery, and electrical industries were faced with a temporary overstocking of products, which also increased their needs for credit (*NCJR*, No 24, 16 December 1986, p.1).

Thus, we can see that the policy of granting credit to rural enterprises was considerably liberalised during the 1980s. The more open access to the state's investment funds clearly created a more favourable environment for the development of rural enterprises. However, the evolution of a credit system was far from unproblematic. The 1980s saw relatively wide fluctuations in credit supply policy. Although access to investment capital was relatively easy at times, macro-economic retrenchment occurred on a number of occasions, and credit supply was reined in. During these periods of credit retraction, rural enterprises were particularly hard hit and found their access to funds severely reduced. In times of difficulty, the state returned to its discriminatory policies towards rural enterprises, instead favouring the more easily controllable state owned sector. Rural enterprise managers were thus unable to plan with any confidence that existing credit supply arrangements would stay in place, a factor which obstructed the even greater development of rural enterprises during this period.

Taxation policy towards rural enterprises

In general, tax policy instruments were used to encourage the growth of collective rural enterprises. The rates of tax paid by the collective sector of rural enterprises had relatively been low. For example, in 1966, the rate of industrial and commercial income tax for commune and brigade enterprises was 20 per cent and the starting point of the levy was 600 *yuan* (Xu Shanda, 1987). In 1979, the starting point was raised to 3,000 yuan. Difficult enterprises run by communes and brigades in old revolutionary bases, minority inhabited areas, and border areas were allowed to enjoy tax reduction or remission for 5 years from 1979. If newly established rural enterprises run by communes or brigades had difficulties in their business operations in the initial stage, they were allowed to enjoy tax reduction or remission for 2 or 3 years (Xu Shanda, 1987). Thus, the rate of industrial and commercial income tax for commune and brigade enterprises was considerably low.

The State Council promulgated some regulations concerning the readjustment of industrial and commercial taxes on enterprises run by rural communes and brigades and they became effective on 1 April 1981 (Xu Shanda, 1987). By this provision, taxes might be continuously reduced or exempted. In some cases this was designed to encourage the development of production by commune and brigade enterprises; for example, products directly serving agricultural production such as chemical fertilizers and pesticides and manufacturing or repairing farm implements. Rural enterprises were also allowed exemption from tax on their industrial and commercial income for two to three years after they were set up.

In 1984 the taxation system was further adjusted. The 'Provisions on Readjusting Industrial and Commercial Tax Rates on Rural Enterprises Run by Townships and Villages on Grass-roots Supply and Marketing Cooperatives' were put into effect from 1st January 1984 (Xu Shanda, 1987). These provisions include the following main points:

As of 1982, the 20 per cent proportional tax rate of the industrial and commercial income tax which rural enterprises paid was gradually changed to the eight-grade progressive tax rate (Mo Tiansong, 1985, pp.31-32). The eight-grade progressive tax rate was implemented in 1982 only on rural enterprises in the suburbs and small towns under county jurisdiction which produced 20 products, including cigarettes, wine and sugar. Only by 1984 was this extended. The purpose of this change was to address the unbalanced development of rural enterprises as well as to legislate a rational tax burden. Industrial and commercial income taxes were levied on all rural enterprises run by communes and brigades according to the eight grade progressive rates with specified minimum rates. The proportional tax rate of 20 per cent was repealed (Mo Tiansong, 1985, pp.31-32).

The eight grade progressive tax rate was different from the proportional tax rate, which was suitable for an enterprise with a smaller income.

85

Correspondingly, a higher tax rate was imposed on an enterprise with a higher income. Thus, taxation corresponds to the profit obtained by an enterprise as well as its ability to shoulder the tax burden. This produced some shift of the tax burden to those enterprises with greater profits and those localities where rural enterprises had developed relatively rapidly together with some shift of the tax burden from those enterprises with smaller profits and localities where rural enterprises had developed relatively slowly. However, in overall terms, the change in the tax burden of rural enterprises was slight (Mo Tiansong, 1985, pp.31-32).

In 1978, rural enterprise profits totalled 9.55 billion yuan, with 640 million yuan of income tax. The effective rate of tax burden was 6.7 per cent (Mo Tiansong, 1985, pp.31-32). In 1983, the state used the eight-grade progressive tax rate to configure the income tax for rural enterprises in the suburbs of large cities and small towns under county jurisdiction. Although the actual burden had increased to 11.49 per cent, compared with 38.13 per cent for the collective enterprises under urban No 2 light industrial system in 1983, this burden was still light (Mo Tiansong, 1985, pp.31-32).

In addition, tax policy towards rural enterprises was ambiguous. For example, as for some special enterprises which needed further tax reductions or remissions, local governments in various provinces, autonomous regions and municipalities could handle their cases according to the following provisions: First, if newly established rural enterprises run by townships or villages had difficulties in their business operations in the initial stage, they could be given a year tax grace period; Second, if enterprises which engaged in the primary processing of agricultural products, small scale hydraulic or thermal power generation, or mining industry found it difficult to pay industrial and commercial taxes, reduced taxes could be imposed on them within a set period (Xu Shanda, 1987). In addition, when townships and villages were hit by natural disasters, industrial and commercial income taxes on rural enterprises could be reduced or remitted within a certain period. Difficult enterprises run by townships and villages in old revolutionary bases, minority inhabited areas, and border areas were allowed to enjoy tax reduction or remission (Xu Shanda, 1987).

Therefore, some local governments had used this ambiguity in tax policy to develop their own strategies towards rural enterprises. They had unilaterally reduced and even exempted income tax on rural enterprises if this measure best suited their own local fiscal interest. My own observation of the situation in China confirms that this practice was widely spread in some counties.

86

After the issuance in April 1985 of the Provisional Income Tax Regulations Governing Collective Enterprises, a system of eight grade progressive taxation was adopted for all collective enterprises (cf. *RMRB*, 20 April 1985, Chen Tesheng, 1986). Under this system the lowest grade was 1,000 yuan, the tax rate on which was 10 per cent, and the highest grade was 200,000 yuan, the tax rate on which was 55 per cent. Newly established township and town enterprises were exempted from paying income tax during a fixed period. Some enterprises which still experienced difficulties after the expiration of the term could continue to enjoy tax exemption or reduction during another fixed period. Spending by a township and town enterprise on public welfare could be listed as expenditure and was entitled to tax exemption, but the total amount was limited to only 10 per cent of its total profit (*Chinese Economic Yearbook 1985*, Sec. 10, p.11).

Therefore, from the above detail it is clear that the state had adopted preferential tax policies with tax reduction or tax exemption measures for collective rural enterprises (township and village owned enterprises). This had undoubtedly played a positive role in the development of rural enterprise. However, tax rates for collective rural enterprises had gradually increased. There had been other tax regulations which had discriminated against rural enterprises. For example, no reduction and remission of industrial and commercial income taxes had been allowed for rural enterprises and other enterprises which competed with large-scale industrial enterprises for raw materials. On the one hand, local governments had exercised the power to reduce and even exempt from income tax on rural enterprises for local interests, whilst on the other, the shortage of fiscal income in local communities and local government funds for welfare work and agricultural funds had also led to the problem of local government exacting a large percentage of profit, collecting excessive charges. I shall analyze this issue in Chapter Seven.

Moreover, China's taxation system had worked in accordance with a commercial ownership type of tax appraisal and collection system, and favoured state owned and collectively owned enterprises over private enterprises. Before June 1988 state owned enterprises fitted into the 55 per cent tax rate bracket. Collective enterprises were adjusted at eight-grade progressive tax bracket where the highest tax rate was only 55 per cent. Individual industrial and commercial firms along with private enterprises had been placed in the tenth grade of progressive tax rates where the highest actual tax rate could be up to 84 per cent. This progressive tax system, administered to the individual industrial and commercial enterprise established in the 1950s was enacted in order to restrict and reform these two sections. This tax system had the following effects.

First large numbers of private enterprises committed tax evasion. According to a survey conducted by the State Tax Bureau, more than 80 per cent of all individually owned industrial and commercial businesses were guilty of tax evasion. In 1988, taxes worth 7 billion yuan were collected from such businesses; but it was estimated that an equal amount was not paid (*BR*, 7-13 August 1989). One informant, engaged in conducting surveys on Shanghai's self-employed, stated that:

> Official tax rates, as well as local 'fees' are often calculated at artificially high levels since the expectation is that everyone is underreporting. Therefore, those who are completely honest will find it difficult to remain in business. Self-employed businessmen of necessity commonly raise prices -- seeming arbitrarily -- to cover these costs (Rosen, 1987, pp.7-8).

Thus, falsified tax returns could be regarded as a part of a systemic flaw rather than as criminal intent on the part of the entrepreneurs. Secondly, faced with mounting tax bills, some private enterprises found it more profitable to reduce production and seek to re-register as 'individually owned enterprises' rather than maintain production and pay the higher tax rate. Thus, continuing to use a 1950s policy of levying high taxes eventually hampered development in the private sector.

In June 1988 the State Council published new tax regulations for private enterprises. In the new regulations, private enterprises had to pay 35 per cent income tax and to use at least 50 per cent of their after-tax profits for production expansion. A 40 per cent personal income tax was levied on the amount private enterprises spent on personal living costs (Nie Lisheng, 1988). New tax regulations tried to offer tax incentives to enterprise expansion and investment of profits. However, private enterprises still suffered from the arbitrary collection of other fees and duties by local government. A private entrepreneur complained that: 'At present, I have to pay 11 kinds of taxes and duties such as business tax, income tax, and taxes for education, construction, real estate, land use as well as industrial and commercial consolidated duties. To be frank, I am taxed too much' (*BR*, 27 February - 5 March 1989, pp.19-22). A number of private enterprises had not been able to bear the burden and had to close down.

In summary, the extension of preferential fiscal policies towards rural enterprises had been one of the main central policies aimed at facilitating the development of rural enterprises. However, despite initially providing a great help for rural enterprises, taxation rates had gradually increased. Rural enterprises had thus fallen foul of the increasing budgetary pressures on central (and local) government. Although the need to increase state finances was a very real one, it is notable that foreign and joint owned ventures had not been subject to an equivalent erosion of special taxation policies, and the further expansion of the rural enterprise sector had certainly not been aided by this move. Given the massive potential long term benefits that rural enterprises could bring to the Chinese economy (as demonstrated in Chapter One), the reduction of tax benefits marked the triumph of short term considerations over long term strategy. Indeed, in almost all respects, the development of the rural enterprise sector had been obstructed by short-termism in central government policy making.

Furthermore, although the collective sector had done relatively well from preferential tax policy, private enterprises were actually penalised by the fiscal system, paying very high taxation rates. This uneven policy had two major effects. Firstly, the expansion of the private sector had obviously been obstructed. Secondly, many private enterprises had officially registered as collective or individually owned. Such an illicit registration was dependent on the collusion of local government officials, which rather than drawing attention to the extent of official corruption in post-Mao China perhaps instead indicates that local cadres were more aware of the need to develop this sector than their central government superiors.

Sources of capital of rural enterprises

In William A.Byrd's research, the sources of capital for rural enterprises was divided into three: household capital, community capital, and enterprise capital (Byrd, 1990, pp.199-203). Household capital was private funds invested directly in rural enterprises by households. It consisted of investment by partners or proprietors, informal loans to private entrepreneurs, purchase of bonds issued by community enterprises, and provision of capital in return for jobs (Byrd, 1990, pp.199-203).

Community capital was investment funds which were determined or strongly influenced by community government, particularly at the township level. This capital consisted of local government budgetary funds for rural enterprise's investment, loans of fiscal revolving funds to rural enterprises, profits from community enterprises pooled by township or village industrial corporations, and banks and rural credit cooperative loans (Byrd, 1990, pp.199-203).

Enterprise capital was the retained profits, depreciation allowances, and other funds of rural enterprises as well as funds provided by other enterprises. Capital from other firms was largely trade credit, of indefinite maturity and highly unstable. The allocations of part of the retained profits and other funds of community enterprises were influenced by the community government, but enterprises could have considerable autonomy in making smaller investments (Byrd, 1990, pp.199-203).

In addition, some capital came from previously existing enterprises such as county industry, later transferred to village and township. William A.Byrd's research (1990, p.202) shows that the state accounted for only a small share of the capital requirements. It was very important for the community to provide initial capital for community enterprises at their founding. The community's share declined as enterprises developed and generated investment funds internally. The role of household capital in financing community enterprises was relatively small.

The information (*Taiyuan Nongye Jingji Xiaoguo* (Taiyuan Agro-Economic Results), No 2, 25 April 1986, pp.8-15) shows that most of the added sources of investments during 1980-83 for the development of rural enterprises were: an average of about 56.5 percent accumulated within the enterprises themselves, about 30.8 percent from bank and credit cooperative loans and 12.6 per cent from other lenders. This indicates that capital accumulated within the enterprises played an important role in sources of added investment in rural enterprises, while the funds from the banks also highly influenced the expansion of rural enterprises.

Over this period, the amount of capital raised by the enterprises themselves basically stayed between 5 and 6 billion yuan and the rate of growth was small, expanding only with township and town enterprises production. About 60 per cent of these loans were assistance loans for circulating capital and investments in fixed assets in township and town enterprises (*Taiyuan Nongye Jingji Xiaoguo*, No 2, 25 April 1986, pp.8-15).

The initial capital for private enterprises came mainly from the following sources:

First, since 1978 the Chinese government adopted a more liberal financial policy towards private enterprise, and the amount of state loans towards private enterprises had risen. According to two surveys of private rural enterprises, state loans accounted for about 50 per cent or 40 per cent of the initial capital for private rural enterprises (Liu Xiaojing, 1988, p.39). Thus, state loans were an important source of the initial capital for private enterprises.

Secondly, previously existing poorly managed small scale collective enterprises had been sold or leased to individuals. The capital from these enterprises became one source of capital formation for private enterprises.

According to some surveys, leased enterprises in 1984 accounted for 18.6 per cent of total private enterprises in Hebei, 30 per cent in Tianjin, and 40 per cent in Liaoning (Liu Wenpu, 1988, pp 27-32).

The third source of initial capital for private enterprise was from credits for the purchase of production materials and prepaid funds. This source was very volatile. A survey of 130 private rural enterprises in 18 provinces indicates that this source accounted for more than 50 per cent of initial capital in 1984, though it dropped to 20 per cent in 1987.

Another important source of initial capital for private enterprise was from individuals and society. I shall further discussed this issue later in this chapter.

In conclusion, capital in both collective and private rural enterprises mainly consisted of household capital, community capital and enterprise capital. State loans played an important role in the formation of the initial capital for both collective and private rural enterprises. The accumulation of individual funds was a less important source of initial capital for collective rural enterprises, but it was a considerable source for private rural enterprises.

Fundraising for rural enterprises

The rise of rural enterprises had increased demand for capital. Capital determined the pace and scale of the development of rural enterprises, while at the same time the development of rural enterprises had affected the circulation of rural capital.

For many years, the development of rural enterprises had relied on community capital, or accumulated capital by the enterprises themselves. However, particularly in the late 1980s, owing to the rapid growth of rural economy, funds from these channels had fallen far short of demands.

After the implementation of the household production responsibility system in Chinese rural areas, the income of Chinese farmers had considerably increased. With the development of the specialized households, in particular, some rich specialized households accumulated several thousand or even tens of thousands of yuan in saving deposits. Total saving deposits in urban and rural areas increased from 21,060 million yuan in 1978 to 307,330 million yuan in 1987 (*China Statistical Yearbook 1988*, Beijing, p.805).

In addition, there was a shift from the collective to peasants' material accumulation in the countryside. Until the end of the 1970s, accumulation in the countryside relied heavily on the collective as a source of capital, equipment and raw materials. Eloquent proof was provided by the following: of the total agricultural output value in 1979, output value of collectively owned enterprises accounted for 79.2 per cent and that of household sideline occupations only 17 per cent (Ling Zhijun, 1986, p.2). After the early 1980s, peasants' personal deposits in credit cooperatives grew at an extremely quick pace, while collective deposits dropped from year to year. In 1985, the peasants personally received in total more than 190 billion yuan, accounting for over 90 per cent of net agricultural income. The collective received only more than 8 billion yuan, accounting for 4 per cent of net agricultural income (Ling Zhijun, 1986, p.2). The investment funds raised by individuals had become available in significant amounts for rural enterprises.

Since late 1980s, rural areas throughout China had developed various capital raising activities for rural enterprise development. This had alleviated the capital shortage to a certain degree. For example, various places had permitted people with either capital or labour to enter the enterprises, investing in shares, importing outside capital, i.e. capital from another area of China or even from foreign countries. In addition, the enterprises could be made more efficient internally in ways like dealing with material overstocks as quickly as possible and pressing for repayment of loans in order to transform unused capital into active capital (cf. Liu Zhihong, 1986, pp.48-50). During the process of capital raising in rural areas across China, both economic and administrative measures have been employed to mobilize the funds.

Fundraising for rural enterprises in rural areas had alleviated the shortage of funds. However, in some places local governments used administrative measures to force farmers to raise funds for rural enterprises. As a result, there had been negative outcomes. First, this had caused blind action in township and village enterprises, construction projects and resulted in half-completed projects. Many enterprises failed to make plans when they got underway and went into operation as soon as they raised a little capital. They placed their hopes for a solution to their capital needs on the flexibility of bank credit and financial investments. Second, because capital collection was assisted by administrative measures, whoever you were poor or rich, you had to participate grudgingly in raising capital. Thus, some of the peasants were not happy with this way.

Conclusion

From 1978 to 1992, China had used diversification as the strategic principle to develop its agricultural economy. Rural enterprises were considered as an important component of a diversified economy, and an important source of state revenue. The government had provided more favourable tax and financial treatment for rural enterprises. As a result, financial and tax policies had provided more favourable financial condition for the development of rural enterprises.

However, tax rates for rural enterprises gradually increased. China's taxation system had still favoured collectively owned rural enterprises over private rural enterprises. In particular, credit supply fluctuated greatly during the 1980s. As a result, this had greatly affected the development of rural enterprises. In particular, from late 1988 to 1991, a retrenchment policy had been implemented, the government reduced loans for rural enterprises, and stopped granting loans to small textile mills, woollen mills, oil refineries, aluminium works, cigarette factories and distilleries (Xinhua in English 12:53 GMT 24 January 1989). Tightening financial policy had produced serious financial difficulty for rural enterprises.

Therefore, fundraising by rural enterprises had become an alternative option. The experience from late 1988 to 1991 shows that rural enterprises will still survive in situation of financial difficulty. Nan Bei (1989, p.3) indicated that: 'the rising tide of fundraising enables us to state one thing without doubt: rural enterprises born amidst the market mechanism have learned to depend on themselves to survive difficulties and crises'. Thus, although the government financial policy will affect the extent of the development of rural enterprises, rural enterprises have an ability to survive and overcome the shortage of funds. With the reform of the financial system, rural enterprises will have more opportunities to obtain funds by different methods.

From 1978 to 1992, China had adopted some policies to improve management in rural enterprises. In the next chapter, I shall discuss how these government policies had influenced management in rural enterprises.

7 Government policies to improve management in rural enterprises

In Chapter Six, I have discussed government financial and taxation policies for rural enterprises. In this chapter, I shall examine the effects of government policy on the management of rural enterprises. Many problems in the management of rural enterprises not only existed but were very serious. In general, management skills in rural enterprises were rather low. Many rural enterprises dropped out of market competition and went bankrupt or closed, and although there were many reasons for this, one of the main reasons was poor management. Therefore, the management of rural enterprises was an important issue. However, the issue of management is a very broad one. In this chapter, I shall mainly concentrate on analyzing local government's role in the management of rural enterprises and the way in which some government policies influenced the management of rural enterprises. In doing so, first, I shall examine the administrative management exercised by township and village governments. Secondly, I shall deal with some government policies towards income distribution in rural enterprises. Finally, I shall analyze the government policy of promoting the quality of production in rural enterprises.

Administrative management systems of rural enterprises

In China the owners of state enterprises belong to all the people. The owners of rural enterprises can be divided into two general categories: town and village governments, and private entrepreneurs. In the state owned enterprises the responsibility for the profits of the assets as well as for risks of the investment of the enterprises was unclear. The loss in state enterprises was often ultimately shifted to the whole of society. However, rural enterprises bore more clear responsibility for the profits of their assets and for the risks involved. The profits and risks of the assets of rural enterprises, especially the investment risks, had to be borne by the members of the villages, townships or individuals.

Since the ownership structures in rural enterprises were different, their administrative management structures also took on different forms. For example, the assets in private rural enterprises belonged to private entrepreneurs, accordingly township and village governments had only indirect control over their management structure. I shall analyze this structure later. By contrast, in traditional collective rural enterprises, township and village governments shared in both rights of ownership and administrative management. Fiscal revenues of townships and villages come largely from rural enterprises in the form of profit remittances and management fees. The profit handed over by township enterprises in sample counties constituted more than 38 per cent of township government revenues, while remittances by township enterprises accounted for 43.6 per cent of township revenues and tax payments by enterprises under other forms of township for 14.3 per cent (Song Lina and Du He, 1990, p.349). Therefore, the income from rural enterprises was a very important source of fiscal revenue of township and village governments.

In addition, William A. Byrd and Alan Gelb's research (1990, pp. 370-376) demonstrated that township and village leaders had personal financial incentives to develop rural enterprises. Personal benefits for township and village leaders were associated with rural enterprise development. First, community leaders' pay varied significantly with the degree of TVP (township, village, private enterprises) development in the community, and this variation was greater for villages and production teams than for townships and towns. Secondly, in the more developed areas of rural enterprises more funds were available for consumption of community government or enterprise resources from cigarettes to banquets to housing construction. Thus, undoubtedly these personal benefits were another incentive for township and village leaders to promote the development of rural enterprises.

The development of rural enterprises, especially collective rural enterprises, was very important for the fiscal incomes of township and village governments as well as for the personal incomes and rewards and career prospects of village and township government leaders. William A. Byrd and Alan Gelb (1990, p.376) pointed out, 'Despite the variation in personal incentives for community government leaders among regions and localities and among community levels, it is clear that everywhere and under almost any circumstance community government leaders have strong incentives to develop the TVP sector (township, village, and private enterprise)'.

Township and village governments had actively aided and supported township enterprises in finance, marketing and technology. Of the township governments surveyed (Du Haiyan, 1988, pp.21-32), 73.0 per cent helped enterprises resolve problems with finances, 49.2 per cent opened a variety of marketing channels for enterprises, and 58.7 per cent provided firms with technological consulting and training. Township and village government run enterprises were the major beneficiaries of this assistance. Song Lina and Du He (1990, pp.342-357) showed that some preferential treatments were given to rural enterprises by township governments. For example, in some cases, township governments have been able to secure for their enterprises some materials that were in short supply. Moreover, the initial capital of rural enterprise largely came from state loans. With the help of local governments, rural enterprises could obtain preferential treatments from banks, industrial and commercial administrative bureaus, and tax and supply departments. Furthermore, local government could help rural enterprise to raise some funds from society in general in order to overcome the shortage of funds in rural enterprises.

However, township and village governments also exercised tight control over rural enterprises, especially township run enterprises and village run enterprises. For example, village and township governments took part in decisions for the selection of township enterprise managers. Township and village government were also directly involved in township enterprises management such as investment, planning, wage levels (Song Lina and Du He, 1990, pp.342-357). This enabled local government in some areas, in particular in backward areas, to extract excessive profits from rural enterprises, and it became clear that some rural enterprises, especially some township owned enterprises, had very low rates of efficiency. As a result, the Chinese government took measures to improve the situation. The main reform took place in traditional collective rural enterprises which were under the direct administrative control of township or village authorities. The main reform aim was to separate government and enterprises and to reduce interference from township and village governments and thereby to increase the efficiency of the enterprises. Reforms however were based on no fundamental change in the status of collective ownership. The main reform measure was to implement the system of contractual responsibility.

Under this contractual responsibility system, all enterprises were contracted to managers, directors, workshops, production groups or to the entire staff. The contractor had management and utilization rights over the property of the enterprise. In other words, the contractor had decision making rights over the manpower, finance and materials of the enterprise as well as over its production, marketing and sales. The contractor was still only the manager of the enterprise, not its owner; contracted responsibility did not entail a transfer of ownership.

Although management and business decisions had largely been left to enterprise directors as a result of the contract system, community governments were still intimately involved in important decisions such as investments, the establishment or dismantling of firms, significant changes in product lines, the appointment of enterprise management, managerial compensation, and bonuses. Community governments could also absorb risk for rural community enterprises and could also finance investments, both directly and through arranging other sources of funding such as bank loans. More generally, they still regarded their collective enterprises as hostile administrative agents. Therefore, although traditional collective rural enterprises had gained more powers after implementing the contract system, township and village governments still deeply controlled township and village enterprises.

The assets of private rural enterprises belonged to private entrepreneurs. Thus, township and village governments had less control over private rural enterprises than over collective rural enterprises, though as a result private rural enterprises could obtain less preferential treatment than collective rural enterprises. However, it was still vital for private rural enterprises to have close relations with local officials since private enterprises still face a discriminating environment as I have discussed in Chapter Two.

Two surveys of private rural enterprises reveal that there was a close relation between local officials and private entrepreneurs. In the first survey (Liu Xiaojing, 1988, p.40), private entrepreneurs in the countryside were divided into the following types according to former occupation: (1) cadres, including the heads of Village Committees, secretaries of Village CCP Committees; (2) former supply and marketing staff in commune and brigade enterprises; (3) retired cadres or former workers or technicians and ordinary urban residents; (4) former specialized households; (5) ex-criminals. This latter was a special category of the entrepreneurs who had been in jail, and some of them were innocent people or victims of Chinese political struggles. The information (Liu Xiaojing, 1988, p.41) shows that the enterprises operated by entrepreneurs of the second, third and fifth category were the largest, or considerably large among private rural enterprises. Enterprises operated by the 'cadre' entrepreneurs type were not as large, but still ranked above the average size. The size of the enterprises operated by ordinary farmers operated was below average. This was due to the fact that most ordinary farmers lacked good functional and social

97

linkages in economics and politics. specialized skills and experiences, and certain other advantages which other types of entrepreneurs enjoyed.

The other survey (*NYJJWT*, No.2, 1989, pp.18-23) also shows that most entrepreneurs of private rural enterprises had special prior experience. Before starting their enterprises, 10.3 per cent had worked in state enterprises, undertakings or departments of government, 11.3 per cent had been servicemen, 7.2 per cent had been teachers, 18.6 per cent had served as supply and marketing staff or as managers in township and village enterprises, and 17.5 per cent had been village cadres. These findings show that there was a close relation between local cadres and private entrepreneurs. As a result, private enterprises, like all other enterprises, were also subject to considerable township and village governments influence. For example, all private rural enterprises needed permission from the community government in order to acquire land, buildings and bank loans. Close personal relationships with community government officials were thus necessary for private enterprises, if they were to flourish.

Therefore, township and village governments were equally important for both private and collective rural enterprises. William A.Byrd and Alan Gelb indicated that 'without the deep involvement of community governments, China's TVP sector could not have grown nearly as rapidly as it did in the late 1970s and early 1980s' (Byrd and Gelb, 1990, p.359). Alan Gelb and Jan Svejnar (1990, p.418) argued that one reason for poor performance of small-scale local industry in Tanzania was local governments had no fiscal or other incentives for ensuring that the ventures were profitable. On the contrary, China's local government had played a very important role in protecting the development of rural enterprises. Township and village governments had dual rights of ownership and management in the traditional collective rural enterprises. In the situation, where the market was not fully operational in China's economy, the protection of rural enterprises by local government was essential. However, the problem remained of how to prevent excessive levies on rural enterprises imposed by township and village governments. I shall discuss this issue later.

Some government measures to improve the income distribution of rural enterprises

In this section, I shall analyze the reform of wage systems within rural enterprises and the role of township and village government in determining wages in rural enterprises. Then I shall examine what kinds of problems of profit distribution existed in rural enterprises and the impact of government policy upon profit distribution.

The reform of the wage system in rural enterprises

The older method of payment was a work point and bonus system. Workers' incomes related to the average income levels of the teams from which the workers came. Enterprises calculated in work points, which were then converted to a money wage according to the workpoint value of their team. However, since their income did not relate to their individual performance, workers in rural enterprises did not have much incentive to work hard.

From 1978 to 1992, the payment system for labour in rural enterprises had been changed. Since the ownership systems of rural enterprises were different, and their profitability varied tremendously, and their means of production ranged from the advanced to the backward, different rural enterprises had adopted different wage systems. The essence of wage system reform in rural enterprises was to find a system that would mobilize worker initiative in production, improve labour productivity, and facilitate production development. Bao Weihuo's research (1986, pp.26-28) shows that the following five wage forms were used in rural enterprises: the piece rate wage system, the time wage system, the contracting income (wage) system, the profit sharing system, the floating wage system.

Within any particular enterprise, it was common for one major wage system to be used in combination with and supplemented by others. Generally speaking, rural enterprises had shifted to the direct payment of workers, and performance based pay. These provided an incentive for work and had improved efficiency in rural enterprises.

Because there had been no unified national system governing income distribution in township and town enterprises, the level of wages in rural enterprises had varied considerably. On average, however, the average wage level in rural enterprises generally was higher than that in agriculture. Although persons engaged in agriculture had greater opportunities to supplement their income from private sideline occupations, even so it was clear that in general rural enterprises paid their workers more than could be earned by farmers. Within rural enterprises, wages of sales staff, technicians and directors were higher than those of workers. The sample from Wuxi and Jieshou revealed these income disparities within rural enterprises. The ratios of average monthly wages, with workers as 1.00, were 1.74 for sales staff, 1.91 for technicians, and 2.07 for directors in Wuxi. In Jieshou the figures are 1.40 for sale staff, 1.96 for technicians and 1.47 for directors (Wu Quhui, Wang Hansheng and Xu Xinxin, 1990, p.330).

The structure of incomes in China in rural enterprises mainly arose out of wages. However, during 1980s some forms of income that were not work-related, such as interest on capital, had produced differential benefits. These forms of income mainly existed in rural private enterprises, and had resulted in a widening of income differential within rural enterprises, especially in private rural enterprises.

No exact statistics are available for the differential of income within the rural private sector, but it was known that some entrepreneurs became millionaires (RMB). The income earned by employers and employees in private enterprises also differed widely. An investigation by Beijing's local government in 1987 revealed that the average monthly salary of employers was 14 times that of employees. The former was 1,600 yuan while the latter was 112 yuan. In Heilongjiang the ratio of average employer's income to average employee's income was 32 to 1, in Shanghai 40 to 1, and in Xian 59 to 1 (*ICM*, February 1988, pp.5-6). In general, therefore, China's entrepreneurs in private rural enterprises sector earned much more than employees in collective rural enterprises; some were among the wealthiest in China.

In sum, since 1978, the wage systems in rural enterprises had been changed to give workers a much greater incentive to work. In general rural enterprises paid their workers more than could be earned by farmers. Wages of sales staff, technicians and directors were higher than those of workers. Income differentials in private rural enterprises were much higher than in collective rural enterprises. Private entrepreneurs earned much more than employees of private and collective rural enterprises.

The reform of profit distribution in rural enterprises

Many problems in profit distribution in rural enterprises existed, and some of these problems were very serious. The main problems were as follows: the extraction by local governments of a large percentage of profit, collecting excessive charges, apportioning numerous expenses, and allowing township and town enterprises to retain little profit. An investigation of 97 rural enterprises (*NMRB*, 13 November 1986, p.2) shows that in the first half of 1986, the enterprises paid a total of 1.047 million yuan in various charges and apportionment, which accounted for 23 per cent of their sales profits. Moreover, these enterprises paid a total of 0.325 million yuan in unlawful charges, accounting for 7.1 per cent of their sales profit (*NMRB*, 13 November 1986, p.2).

The shortage of local government funds was the main reason for local government exacting a large percentage of profit and collecting excessive charges. Since 1978, there had been an increase in local government's expenditures on rural education, health, family planning, subsidies for military recruitment and militia training, and subsidies for households with difficulties, old-age homes, and other social welfare activities. This high level of social expenditure had led to encroachments on a large portion of rural enterprises profits.

William A.Byrd and Alan Gelb (1990, pp. 376-379) found that the problem of fiscal predation was more serious in backward areas than in well-endowed areas. The reasons are as follows: first, in better-off areas there was a strong base of existing community enterprises, and so most community governments were in a relatively comfortable financial situation. Secondly, these areas had more personal incomes and bank deposits which could be used for loans to rural enterprises. As a result, more funds were available for reinvestment to develop rural enterprises. By contrast, in backward areas the development of rural enterprises was much more limited. The difficult financial situation of community governments made them draw funds from community enterprises for public expenditures regardless of the enterprises' profitability and ability to pay. Even when firms were losing money, they still had to make payments to community governments in order to meet urgent and largely fixed public expenditure needs.

Due to the lack of unified standards for profit retention and distribution, practice differed widely from place to place. For example, the Beijing Municipal Region had stipulated that township and town enterprise profits were distributed according to a '4:3:3' ratio. The enterprise retained 40 per cent, handed in 30 per cent to township government (or village government) to be used primarily for the support of agriculture, and delivered the remaining 30 per cent to the township or village economic organizations (enterprise companies) to be used to expand production or build new enterprises (Bao Weihe, 1986, pp.20-22). In Simen Town, Yutao City, Zhejiang Province, a regulation was adopted using a 'double 3-7' ratio in the distribution of after-tax township and town profit, in which 70 per cent of after-tax profits was retained by the enterprises for use in expanded production and 30 per cent was given over to the town industrial bureau. Of the profit handed in, 70 per cent was retained by the bureau to use in supporting the renovation of older enterprises and the building of new township and town enterprises, while 30 per cent was given to the town government to use in the construction of small market towns and other expenditures of a social nature (Bao Weihe, 1986, pp.20-22).

Pertaining to the problem of township enterprises' heavy social burden, low profit retention, and other problems, the State Economic Commission's agriculture, animal husbandry, and fishery departments jointly issued a circular entitled 'Several Suggestions on the Question of Township Enterprises' Profit Distributions' (*NMRB*, 22 December 1986, p.1). Enterprises should be allowed to retain a minimum of 60 per cent of the net profits. Village and township leaders should respect the right of the enterprises to operate their businesses and utilize their funds autonomously. Enterprises should have the right to reject equalitarianism and indiscriminate transfer of resources or unreasonable apportionment. However, the community's or the region's economic interests could undermine the authority of the central government and effectiveness of its functioning departments. Since most township and village governments had the shortage of funds, the pressure on them to extract excessive funds from rural enterprises was immense.

Some scholars had provided some good suggestions to prevent fiscal predation by township and village governments. William A.Byrd and Alan Gelb (1990, p.386) suggested that the size of community government and the number of cadres should be reduced to correspond better with local community resources, and that some expenditures on activities such as primary education which were important to national objectives should be included in the state budget. These were indeed good suggestions. However, China's agricultural investment from central government was still limited, and this means that local governments required rural enterprises to turn over a large portion of funds from their profits for the development of agriculture (Zhang Xiaoli and Liu Yaguang, 1986, p.2). In addition, China's state budget itself required the turning over of a large portion of funds from the profits of rural enterprises. Therefore, although China's central government had formulated some measures to reduce the financial burden of rural enterprises, some problems of profit distribution still remained in rural enterprises.

Government policy towards product quality of rural enterprises

In general, product quality of rural enterprises was low. According to an investigation in some township and town enterprises in Jiangsu and Shandong in 1986 (*ZGXZQYB*, 15 January 1986 p.3), in many enterprises awareness of quality was quite poor. Emphasis was given to output and profits, not to quality.

There were either no standards in product manufacturing or work was not done according to standards. Product quality was not stable. For example, of 16 products in Wuxi selected by the Bureau of Standards Jiangsu, only 7, or 44 per cent, were up to standard (*ZGXZQYB*, 15 January 1986, p.3). According to this analysis, the proportion of products up to standard throughout the province was estimated at approximately 50 per cent. In Yantai, Shandong Province 1,402 products from 990 enterprises were examined and 67.2 per cent were found to be up to standard. Problems in product quality in some firms, particularly food enterprises, were even more serious. Of 162 products in 140 enterprises throughout the province, only 45 per cent were up to standard (*ZGXZQYB*, 15 January 1986, p.3).

Considerable numbers of enterprises lacked even the most basic quality guarantees, and did not have the capacity to manufacture products that were up to standard. For example, in Jiangsu, over 50 per cent of industrial products in township and town enterprises were substandard. Most enterprises were 'imperfect in four areas', that is, in blueprints, standards, technology, and structure, so it was very difficult to guarantee quality. In Shandong 2,078 enterprises were investigated. Of these, 361, or 17.4 per cent, lacked blueprints and technology; 252, or 12.1 per cent, lacked an inspection system; and 503, or 24.7 per cent, had unsound examination and measuring methods (*ZGXZQYB*, 15 January 1986, p.3).

A few enterprises even used inferior material and did shoddy work, manufactured goods in a rough and slipshod way and even palmed off inferior goods as brand name products. For example, in Yantai, in 1985, 870 bicycles, 725 cartons of cigarettes, and 46,000 bottles of alcohol and beverages, were found, all with fake name brands and which came from other parts of the country (*ZGXZQYB*, 15 January 1986, p.3). Circumstances such as these had been discovered in quality inspections throughout the country.

In addition, below the village level (including cooperative enterprise, joint households and individual enterprises) there was basically no one in charge of product quality (*ZGXZQYB*, 15 January 1986, p.3).

Thus, the problem of product quality in rural enterprises was quite serious. In response to the problems, the State Economic Commission, Ministry of Agriculture, Animal Husbandry, and Fishery and the State Industry and Commerce Administration formulated 'Opinions on Strengthening Product Quality Management Work in Township and Town Industries':

All township and town enterprises must do more to correct their administrative ideology, adhere earnestly to the principle of 'quality is number one' and strive to improve management and administration, raise economic results, and be concerned with preventing pollution of the environment (*ZGXZQYB*, 12 March 1986, P.3).

'The Opinions' called for township and town enterprises administrative departments to establish quality management organs to work in conjunction with industrial management departments and industrial and commercial administration organs and thereby to strength management and supervision over product quality. 'The opinion' suggested focusing on industrial enterprises at the township (town) level and key village run industrial enterprises. The main concern for industrial enterprises below the village level was to strengthen quality supervision.

This account shows that China's central government were aware of the importance of product quality, and had taken some steps to improve product quality in rural enterprises. However, as the author observed in some of China's regions in 1980s, enforcement had been weak since local officers paid more attention to jobs and growth than to product quality and other standards.

Conclusion

From 1978 to 1992, fiscal revenues of township and village governments largely depended on the incomes from rural enterprises. In addition, there was a very close interest relation between township and village government leaders and the development of rural enterprises. Furthermore, the development of rural enterprises had played a very important role in increasing the incomes of rural community members and solving the problem of rural surplus labour. Thus, township and village governments actively defended the interests of rural enterprises and promoted the development of rural enterprises. In China, rural enterprises were lower in status than state owned enterprises, and as a result, they obtained less preferential treatments from central government. Under this situation, it was essential for rural enterprises to obtain some protection for township and village governments.

The different wage forms had been used in rural enterprises. The reform of the wage systems in rural enterprises had given workers a greater incentive to work. Rural enterprises paid their workers more than could be earned by farmers. Wages of sales staff, technicians and directors, especially private entrepreneurs were higher than workers. These income differentials may be widened since private rural enterprises continue to develop rapidly and private rural enterprises have less control over wage differentials from township and village governments.

The shortage of fiscal income and local government funds for welfare work and agricultural funds had led to the problem of local government exacting a large percentage of profit, collecting excessive charges. Although China's central government had implemented a policy of reducing the financial burden of rural enterprises, some problems of profit distribution had remained. Product quality in rural enterprises was still low. Although China's central government had implemented a policy to improve product quality in rural enterprises from 1978 to 1992, enforcement had been weak.

From 1978 to 1992, China's government adopted some measures to promote technology in rural enterprises. In the next chapter, I shall examine how these policies had influenced technological progress in rural enterprises.

8 Government policies to promote technology in rural enterprises

In the former chapter, I have discussed government policies to promote management in rural enterprises. In this chapter, I shall examine government policies to promote technological progress in rural enterprises since 1978.

There has been much published discussion on the economic aspects of technological change. However, there has been considerable difference of opinion on several issues such as the causes and effects of technological change. For example, on the plus side, as a result of technological changes more and better durable consumer goods become available to most people, however, on the debit side, pessimists argued that automation could lead to unemployment and more or less enforced leisure on a large scale. However, most economists have agreed on the importance of technological change as a very important source of economic growth. Paul A. David's research on the American and British experience in the nineteenth century indicated that a single, distinct technological innovation may lead to aggregate economic growth (Paul A. David, 1975). Kazushi Ohkawa and Henry Rosovsky found that institutional changes as well as experience with new technologies stimulated Japan's social capability to import and eventually improve on advanced foreign production methods (Kazushi Ohkawa and Henry Rosovsky, 1973). Despite political disruptions, China has also illustrated the important role of science and technology development on economic and social development. Tony Saich's research demonstrated that 'there is a clear recognition of the important role that science and technology plays in achieving economic and social objectives', and 'the process of reform has led to the realization that much greater attention must be paid to the process of science and technology development itself' (Tony Saich, 1989, pp.156-158).

The concern in this chapter is to examine one aspect of the impact of science and technology development on Chinese economic development -- the impact on rural enterprises from 1978 to 1992. In so doing, first I shall analyze technology in rural enterprises. Then I shall analyze government technological strategy before and after 1978. Next I shall examine the progress of technology in rural enterprises. Finally I shall analyze the prospects for technological progress in rural enterprises.

Technology in rural enterprises

In China's rural enterprises, old and new equipment existed side by side in most rural enterprises. The technological modernization process was more advanced in the coastal regions, but even in the coastal regions many rural enterprises still used old technology and equipment. Less than 20 per cent of the equipment was made in the 1970s and 1980s; over 60 per cent was made in the 1950s and 1960s; and about 20 per cent was basically primitive hand-operated equipment (*ZGXZQYB*, 15 January 1986, p.3). The quality of workers and staff was low. The capacity of these enterprises to develop new products on their own was also extremely limited. This means that they had to depend on technological assistance from outside to make the fullest use of technology. Lack of local technological capacity arose from the absence of any in-house research and design facilities. Assistance was sought by these enterprises from either large enterprises or from research institutes or universities. The proportion of technically trained personnel was only one-tenth that in state-run enterprises. The quality of 70-90 per cent of all products was lower than the products of state owned enterprises. There were more products of medium and inferior quality, more old-style products, and fewer new products (*JRSB*, 19 December 1988, p.1).

One survey (Bi Guohua and Bao Yonghong, 1989, p.4) shows that in the sample enterprises, the equipment came from the following sources: 37 per cent was new equipment which was ordered from the factories; 29 per cent was bought from the market; 13 per cent was old equipment bought from factories; 10 per cent was the equipment which had been retired from state-run factories; 9 per cent was made by themselves; 2 per cent was imported from overseas. The information (Bi Guohua and Bao Yonghong, 1989, p.4) indicated that only 10 per cent of these sample enterprises' equipment was made in the 1980s. Most equipment in sample enterprises was out-of-date.

In summary, the level of technology in most rural enterprises was inferior. The low level of technology was one of the main reasons of the low quality of products.

Government technological strategies for rural enterprises

From 1955 to 1957, China launched a large-scale agricultural cooperative movement. Commune and brigade enterprises, the predecessors of rural enterprises, began to emerge and develop on the basis of collective sideline production.

During the Great Leap Forward, the techniques strategy was the approach which entailed primary but temporary emphasis upon small-scale, labour intensive methods of production within the framework of long-term priority for large-scale and capital intensive techniques (Carl Riskin, 1971, pp.245-273). The Great Leap Forward policy attempted rapid rural industrialization through mass mobilization and the use of primitive techniques. Because premature expansion of small plants led to waste and confusion, many commune and brigade enterprises were closed during the retrenchment of 1960 to 1962. But as agricultural conditions stabilized and the opportunity cost of small scale industrial ventures declined, official policy began once again to encourage local industrial development. The volume of the resources devoted to commune and brigade enterprises had expanded steadily since 1963. Careful attention to pilot projects, cost reduction, and quality control had led to improved results (Rawski, 1980).

As research by Samuel P.S.Ho (1986, p.40) indicated, rural industry differed from urban industry because it existed primarily to serve agriculture and local markets, consists mostly of small plants using primitive or intermediate technology, and depends on local resources. However, after 1978 although China still demanded that rural enterprises supported agriculture, rural enterprises had been considered as a policy of strategic significance in solving rural surplus labour and as an important source of the peasants' increased income (cf. *RMRB*, 19 May 1984). Technological strategy placed emphasis upon appropriate technology. Although most rural enterprises were still small-scale and engaged in labour intensive methods of production, the State had not restricted rural enterprises wishing to become large-scale and capital intensive. An important official report clearly indicated this strategy:

108

Commune and brigade enterprises should not arbitrarily seek advanced equipment and technology without considering their actual conditions, nor should they be contented with their backwardness in technology and refuse to advance. They should adopt appropriate technology on the basis of their respective salient features (The Minister of Agriculture, Animal Husbandry and Fishery and the Ministry's Leading Party Group. (1984), *SWB/FE*, 26 March).

The report suggested that the State should adopt a policy favourable to the replacement of very old equipment. The rate of depreciation on old fixed assets might be raised appropriately. With regard to the use of after-tax profits, the report suggested that priority should generally be given to technological transformation.

In addition, the report encouraged cooperation in technology between state enterprises and rural enterprises, and between scientific research departments, colleges or institutions of higher training and rural enterprises. At the same time, the report offered some suggestions to improve the lack of technological personnel in rural enterprises. This will be analyzed below.

Faced with the reality of a backward and generally inefficient domestic science and technology system, Chinese leaders had been engaged in an effort to re-structure their research sector and modernize indigenous science and technology capabilities since 1978 (cf. Denis F. Simon, 1987). The March 1978 National Science Conference in Beijing was a milestone in the reform of science policy. Its main purpose was to announce publicly the government and party policy of encouragement and support of science and technology. A major speech by Deng Xiaoping reiterated the concept of science as a productive force and scientists as workers. However, the fundamental reform of the science and technology management system was made by the March 1985 Central Committee Decision. The reforms proposed in the 'Decision on the Reform of the Science and Technology Management System' (Xinhua in 19 March 1985, *FBIS*-PRC, 21 March 1985, pp.1-9) represented a major break with past practices, by changing the method of funding research institutes, encouraging the commercialization of technology and the development of a technology market and rewarding individual scientists. It was envisaged that most research institutes would support themselves through partnerships, mergers, joint ventures, or other appropriate and mutually agreeable means. The ultimate goal was to encourage exchange and cooperation and to break down the compartmentalization characterizing China's research and development structure.

The reform of the science and technology management system had very important implications for the technological development of rural enterprises. As I shall discuss later, increasing numbers of technological personnel had worked in rural enterprises. Technological cooperation between state enterprises and rural enterprises and between research institutes and universities and rural enterprises had taken place. A technology market and the commercialization of technology in the late 1980s were developed to encourage the transfer of technology and the transformation of research results into products and services. Thus, rural enterprises had opportunities to get technology through the technological market and via the system for the transfer of technology.

Various technological fairs had operated from 1978 to 1992. For example, Jilin Province signed a number of contracts and agreements on technological cooperation and transfers in the first Northeast China technological cooperation fair on 26 April 1986. The total transaction volume reached 40m yuan (*SWB/FE/W* 7 May 86, Changchun, Jilin provincial service 10:30 GMT 26 April 1986). According to statistics released by 17 departments in 22 provinces, autonomous regions and municipalities, about 87,000 contracts, worth 2.06 billion yuan were signed at the market in 1986. China had 5,000 organizations handling technological business activities, while 10,000 state-run and 10,000 privately-run research institutes became more active in the country's commodity and technological markets (*SWB/FE/W*, 3 June 1987, Xinhua in English 07:29 GMT 27 May 1987).

Private scientific research institutes had been allowed to be established since 1978. According to statistics, China had 10,000 private scientific research institutes with 800,000 employees in 1987, which made profits by selling the application of their discoveries. 308 private scientific research institutes located in 20 cities had technologically aided 221 small and village and township enterprises from 1985 to 1986 (*SWB/FE/W*, 16 December 1987, Xinhua in English 12:06 GMT 2 December 1987).

Some private scientific research institutes had set up experimental plants in rural areas. One experimental factory was jointly launched by a private institute and a village in Dalian. With the help of the private institute, the factory, which went into operation in 1985 with an investment of 1.5 million yuan, sold its products to a dozen major cities. The institute was based in a rural area and had helped 30 rural enterprises become profitable (*SWB/FE/W*, 16 December 1987, Xinhua in English 12:06 GMT 2 December 1987).

China's leadership also expected rural enterprises to play an important role in the development of the export-oriented economy (*CD*, 19 December 1987). Some rural enterprises in coastal areas had engaged in the processing of imported material, assembly of imported parts and compensation trade. In 1985, more than 8,000 township enterprises nationwide earned foreign exchange through exports. They produced 20 major categories, more than 10,000 varieties of products sold in nearly a hundred nations worldwide, and earned more than $4 billion, 15.5 per cent of the nation's total foreign exchange earnings in 1985 (Xu Yu, 1987, pp.16-20). Some rural enterprises in coastal areas had also cooperated with foreign businesses. This will be discussed later. As a result, such enterprises had an opportunity to use foreign advanced technology.

Because the development of rural enterprises in China was uneven, different regions had been given different strategies for technological improvement. In the interior and in other regions where rural enterprises were relatively underdeveloped, technological improvement had emphasized the promotion of traditional arts and crafts. But in the coastal areas where rural enterprises were relatively advanced, input of more advanced technology had taken place. This could further widen the regional imbalances in the development of rural enterprises.

From 1989 to 1992, the Chinese leadership had emphasized the development of state enterprises. Despite this, Chinese official documents still supported technological progress in rural enterprises. One document called for the government to organize and guide technological progress, staff training, and to create the conditions for rural enterprises to recruit skilled personnel and import advanced technology (*XHYB*, No.6, 1990, p.86).

However, it should be noted that the support and favourable conditions for technological progress in official documents were given more to township and village collective run enterprises than to private rural enterprises. This was due to the discrimination against private enterprises and to the low stature of private enterprises.

Since 1978, the most important promotion of the application of modern science and technology to rural enterprises was the State introduced 'Spark Plan'. In essence, the program was intended to replace the outdated equipment in rural areas by modern factory methods. This will be discussed below.

To sum up this section, during the 1980s technological strategy for rural enterprises had been changed from the emphasis on small-scale, labour-intensive methods of production and primitive technology to the use of appropriate technology. The reform of the science and technology management system had given rural enterprises opportunity to obtain advanced technology.

The open door policy and the policy of encouraging higher quality of products in rural enterprises had important implications for the promotion of technological progress in rural enterprises. The Chinese Government had also given some practical support towards technological progress of rural enterprises.

The progress of technology in rural enterprises

In this section, I shall examine technological progress in rural enterprises. This includes the following aspects: the 'Spark Plan' towards rural enterprises; technological personnel in rural enterprises; cooperation in technology between state enterprises and rural enterprises and between research institutes and universities and rural enterprises.

The Spark Plan (Xinghuo Jihua)

The Spark Plan was initiated by the State Science and Technology Commission in March 1985. The plan, which derived its name from a Chinese metaphor that said a single spark can start a prairie fire, aimed at introducing modern science and techniques to the rural districts through the medium of technological demonstration centres with the object of accelerating economic growth in the countryside. The Spark Plan was proposed in the spirit of the resolution by the Central Committee to restructure the science and technology system, and was aimed at invigorating the local economy (Liu Zhongkui, 1986, pp.1-3). The targets of the plan during the Seventh Five-year Plan were: (1) to develop 100 complete sets of technological equipment suitable for the countryside and the town and township enterprises, and put them into batch production; (2) to help establish 500 model town and township enterprises and provide them with complete technology and production techniques and methods of standard management, product design and quality control; (3) to train a number of educated youths and grassroots cadres for towns and townships every year so that they could master one or two advanced technologies suitable for their own areas and obtain some knowledge of modern management (Wu Mingyu, 1986).

The Spark Plan introduced technology of a higher level in China's eastern seaboard to help produce better quality goods for the export market. Assistance was given to help the central part of China manufacture goods for the domestic market, so as to lay the foundation for starting an export-oriented economy. Underdeveloped western China was where the plan could help most by

112

introducing techniques to enable millions of rural households to become well-to-do. The plan helped enterprises in western China to enter into cooperation with those in the central and eastern parts of the country so that they could turn out market goods with local characteristics.

A whole series of new measures were adopted: all projects to be listed as Spark Plan had to undergo feasibility studies by experts and were no longer started up after nothing more than a simple administrative investigation. Technical projects for rural enterprises to be listed had to have a technical institute, scientific research unit, or large or mid-sized enterprises to look to, in order to assure that the project was both advanced and appropriate. Some projects were not arranged through administrative channels but through public announcements in newspapers which solicited technological personnel and had the support of the state for loans. Capital accumulation channels were expanded. Bonds and stocks were issued, and enterprises linked up to accumulate capital. All forms of venture capital investment and leasing system had been tried (Li Shuzhong, 1987, pp.14-16).

Many kinds of technology transfer systems had been established. Compensation had been paid for the transfer of technological contracts and markets for information and technology had been created. For example, a total of 87 out of 98 counties and prefectures had started rural technology markets, resulting in the spread of appropriate technology through a large segment of rural enterprises (Li Shuzhong, 1987, pp.14-16). Human resource exchange agencies had also been established. Science and technology workers had been given incentives to go to work in rural enterprises.

These new methods had provided favourable conditions for the implementation of the Spark Plan. Between 1985 and 1987, the state put up 360 million yuan in support of the Spark Plan. The capital accumulation in the different regions reached 1.9 billion yuan (Li Shuzhong, 1987, pp.14-16). These funds had been used to develop technological application in 10 areas: new modes in the feed industries and for storing and shipping their products; processing technology for preserving freshness at the point of production; technology for the comprehensive use of farm, forestry and local products; development of rural township construction materials; production technology for small-scale mining excavation, extraction, primary processing and manufacturing; broadened utilization of new technology and materials; product lines for heavy industrial production; coordinated regional development; export commodities; and development of small-scale production installation technology and training of installation personnel (Li Shuzhong, 1987, pp.14-16).

The work of personnel training had gone forward as well. Training centers had been set up all around the country; and 1.05 million young peasants with intermediate education levels had participated (Li Shuzhong, 1987, pp.14-16).

After three years' implementation, the Spark Plan had achieved visible success. By the end of 1988, 5,100 projects were completed, increasing output value by 11.2 billion yuan and profits and taxes delivered to the state by 3.6 billion yuan, earning 1.6 billion yuan in foreign exchange, and enabling the input-output ratio to reach 1:5 (*SWB/FE/W*, 22 March 1989, Xinhua in Chinese 15:08 GMT 6 March 1989).

Thus, the implementation of the Spark Plan gained some successes for the improvement of technology in some rural enterprises. However, this program had been far from adequate compared with the number and size of rural enterprises in all China. As noted above, most rural enterprises still lacked sufficient technological personnel, and use out-dated facilities, often procured from state and collective enterprises that had upgraded their technological base. Although the reliance on second hand equipment was a cheap way of obtaining productive capacity in the short run, much of it was highly inefficient, and highly energy consumptive. Thus, although the Spark Plan marked an important step in the right direction, much work still remained to be done to improve the technology of rural enterprises.

Technological personnel

Since 1978, some enterprises faced bankruptcy and some went out of business. The most important reason for their failure was the lack of competent managers and technicians. For instance, Nanggong County in Hebei, Chuiyang township spent 110,000 yuan on a set of advanced shoe-making equipment. Yet none of the seven 'technicians' it successively hired from outside at a high salary had mastered the entire spectrum of shoe technology and they were particularly inadequate when it came to design. The enterprise failed 4 months after it went into business (Chen Qingzhong, 1986, pp.10-11). Professional technicians made up a small proportion of the workers in rural enterprises. In 1986, 1,520,000 rural enterprises surveyed had only 630,000 professional technicians, an average of 0.4 technicians for one enterprise. For all the 43.91 million rural workers, technicians accounted for only 0.7 per cent of the total. The per centage for state enterprises was 8.8 per cent (*CD*, 3 November 1987).

In order to improve the situation of lack of technological personnel in rural enterprises, a Chinese official document suggested that the following steps should be taken: First, the education department had to include rural enterprises' requirements for personnel in the plan for developing vocational education and gradually establish professional schools for training staff members and staff. Secondly, the state had to assign some university and college graduates to rural enterprises. Thirdly, rural enterprises had to be allowed to give proper titles to their technological personnel by referring to the criteria promulgated by the state in order to encourage the staff members and workers to become competent personnel through self-study (*SWB/FE,* 2 October 1987, Xinhua in English 17:05 GMT 27 September 1987).

Meanwhile, the Chinese government had also accelerated, especially since 1985, the introduction and training of technological and management personnel for township and town enterprises. According to an investigation in 1985 involving 23 provinces and municipalities, a total of 65,000 capable people were recruited by township and town enterprises and 600,000 technological and management personnel were trained. A special characteristic of the work to cultivate talented personnel had been the operation of educational and training programs for staff and workers at various levels, through various channels, and in various forms (Chen Te-sheng, 1986).

The State also adopted a more liberal policy which allowed technological personnel to work in rural enterprises in their spare time. In certain big cities such as Shanghai and Beijing, groups of scientific technological personnel traveled to suburbs from downtown either by bus or bicycle on Sunday to use their spare time to help rural enterprises develop new products, tackle technological problems, and train workers. This was very useful in solving the problems of technology in rural enterprises.

However, very few technological personnel in state enterprises could settle in rural areas and work in rural enterprises. The main reasons were as follows: first, some leaders of the state departments feared that once the scientific and technological personnel went to work in rural enterprises, they would become their rivals, and that the scientific and technological personnel going to work in rural enterprises and getting higher wages could affect the stability and ideology of technological personnel who still worked in their departments.

Second, the personnel were afraid of losing their 'iron rice bowls'. In China, state employees received a broad array of subsidies for basic consumption goods, services, and other benefits that were not provided to farmers. In 1978 these included subsidies for grain, vegetable oils, and subsidiary foods, for housing, retirement, death, maternity, disability, injury, and some types of health benefits and labour insurance fees, etc. These subsidies in 1978 totalled 528 yuan per year per employee or 82 per cent of the average wage (Lardy, 1983, pp.163-164). If they went to rural enterprises to work, they would lose these subsidies.

Third, there was an ideological and political reason why very few technological personnel work in rural enterprises. As Denis F. Simon's research indicated, political cadres saw themselves as being displaced by science and technological personnel. Party officials felt insecure in granting these individuals more authority and independence, especially since they threaten the party's own claims to be the main purveyor of truth and knowledge in society (Simon, 1987, p.142). Technological personnel were worried about other people criticizing them by saying that their purpose in going down to work in the township and town enterprises was to 'make big money'. In some cases, these individuals had been accused of extortion and blackmail by jealous individuals who had not had such opportunities available to themselves (*FBIS*-PRC, 20 July 1984, p.3).

It would be very difficult for the enterprises to train this large number of workers by themselves. The official proposal was that 1 per cent of the tax money turned over to the State from rural enterprises, about 2 billion yuan, be used to train workers in rural enterprises. However, this was still not an adequate solution.

Cooperation in technology

Before cooperation in technology is discussed, it is necessary to give a brief description of the system of China's science and technology. An unreformed Soviet system of science and technology structure, which operated in China until the late seventies, was unsuccessful in providing a sufficient, consistent link between the research and productive sectors (Saich, 1989, pp.34-35). Moreover, sources of technology were different for various parts of the industrial spectrum. Nation and province level enterprises received their technological inputs mainly from national science and technology institutes and through imports. Lower-level enterprises were not completely cut off from these sources, but the bottom of the industrial pyramid derived its technological advancement mainly from a process of internal diffusion. Advanced science and technology were available mainly at higher levels. Intermediate science and technology were available for the middle levels, while the lower levels mainly got technological knowledge from a popular-based extension network (Sigurdson, 1977, p.77). Thus, rural enterprises could only obtain inputs of low technology. If rural enterprises wanted to obtain advanced technology, it was necessary for them to cooperate with state enterprises, research institutes and universities.

Since 1978, technological cooperation had been encouraged by the Chinese government, as the following statement illustrated:

In the past two years, the commune and brigade enterprises in some localities have invited scientists and technicians from various scientific research departments, colleges and institutions of higher training, and designing departments to work as their advisers, assume the task of manufacturing new products on a trial basis, and apply the results from scientific research in production. This practice has helped the enterprises acquire many new techniques and turn out many new products. This has not only quickened the pace in turning science and technology into an actual productive force and closely linked scientific research with production, but has also solved the problem of weak technological forces in commune and brigade enterprises. Efforts must be made earnestly to sum up and propagate our experience in this respect (The Minister of Agriculture, Animal Husbandry and Fishery and the Ministry's Leading Party Group, *SWB/FE* 26 March 1984).

Cooperation efforts between research institutes or universities and rural enterprises and between state enterprises and rural enterprises had gone further. They took varied forms, took place at different levels and developed in different directions.

Transfer of technology was a very common form of cooperation in technology. Both 'vertical' and 'horizontal' transfers of technology had taken place from foreign countries, research institutes and universities to rural enterprises or from state enterprises to rural enterprises. For example, a knitting mill in Jiangyin County, Jiangsu Province had less than 100 workers before 1981. After cooperating with the Jiangsu Import and Export Company of Knitting Products, and importing advanced foreign technology in 1981, by 1986 the mill produced 29.95 million yuan and earned $5.6 million foreign exchange. The scale of the mill increased to about 1,000 workers and 6 million yuan of fixed capital in 1987 (Yan Yingeong, 1987). This form of technology transfer was most suitable for those technologies that were not very sophisticated and could be easily adopted. Research institutes or universities were responsible for furnishing the enterprises with the technology and solving the problems arising during production, but they did not take part in the management of the enterprises. The transfer of technology to previously non-industrialized areas

117

was a very important part of the policies to promote the development of rural areas and thereby reduce poverty. Localities which had already started their industrialization would continue to be dependent on technology transfer in order to upgrade their industrial capability and move into the manufacture of more complicated products.

In the process of the transfer of technology, big state enterprises in a number of places played a very important role in promoting technological cooperation with rural enterprises. Cooperation between urban state enterprises and rural enterprises took place in two different forms. On the one hand, state enterprises sent personnel and equipment to the places where new rural enterprises were to be set up. On the other hand, technological personnel were trained in state enterprises. For example, in Changsha, Hunan, 49 urban enterprises cooperated with 108 rural factories to manufacture 267 products, increasing the output value to 130m yuan in 1986. The rural enterprises acquired 1,995 technicians, 16.6m yuan and 385 machines through the cooperation, while offering land, labour and profit-sharing with their urban counterparts (*SWB/FE/W*, 5 February 1986, Xinhua in English 07:52 GMT 23 January 1986).

While helping rural enterprises to improve their technology and increase their incomes, urban enterprises had also expanded production and developed new and competitive products through cooperation. For example, Changlegang village in Changsha County used to grow only rice, sweet potatoes and hot peppers in the past while rich deposits of tin ore lay idle nearby. The village and a geological institute in Changsha set up a factory in July 1986. With techniques and equipment provided by the institute, the village produced 250 tons of finished ore worth 400,000 yuan. After recovery of investment, the village shared profits of 100,000 yuan. The 40 families in the village averaged an additional income of 1,300 yuan. When the provincial embroidery factory lacked female labour in 1985, it signed contracts with a nearby town. The 700 rural women, processing supplied materials in their homes, helped the factory complete export tasks, while earning about 40 yuan per capita each month (*SWB/FE/W*, 5 February 1986, Xinhua in English 07:52 GMT 23 January 1986).

There was also cooperation between research institutes and universities and rural enterprises. Some research institutes and universities sent their experts to the enterprises to work as technological advisers according to the needs of specific enterprises, thus providing technological advice and services in relation to its production. In addition, research institutes and universities trained students majoring in subjects requested by rural enterprises, and offer training classes in business management for factory directors and managers. For example, Liaoning province had developed a project to spread advanced technology

118

through a network involving three counties, 20 townships and 100 villages. The three-year program was carried out on an experimental basis in Fuxing, Kazuo and Haicheng counties in 1982. The three counties trained more than 226,000 people through 1,100 technology courses between 1983 and 1985 (*SWB/FE/W*, 29 January 1986, Xinhua in English 09:05 GMT 16 January 1986). In 1985 some 1,300 experts, technicians and various other types of professional personnel were invited to work in the three counties and 20 townships. They conducted surveys on local natural resources, helped in working out development plans and spread technology by training personnel (*SWB/FE/W*, 29 January 1986, Xinhua in English 09:05 GMT 16 January 1986). The example from Liaoning Province shows that training programs were improving, and in a few cases, the technological expertise in rural enterprises had improved. However, on a national scale, the level of personnel and technology transfer remained relatively low, and was a key impediment to the long term development of an efficient and more productive rural enterprise sector.

Some research institutes and universities also cooperated with rural enterprises to undertake joint research projects. Research institutes or universities provided technology while rural enterprises provided buildings, manpower, capital and other facilities. After the results of one project were put into production, other joint research projects could be planned and arranged according to the need of the enterprises. As a result, the enterprises were able to develop new products at different times. For example, the three counties mentioned above established ties with over 160 colleges, research units and industrial enterprises to absorb modern technology. The 20 townships achieved good economic results owing to the spread of 233 new technology items in 1985. By the end of October, they had produced a total industrial and agricultural output value of 553.29 million yuan -- a 57.73 per cent increase over the same period of 1984 (*SWB/FE/W*, 29 January 1986). Thus, it was a good way to promote the cooperation between rural enterprises and research institutes and universities. In so doing, on the one hand, research institutes and universities could gain funds by providing technology for rural enterprises. On the other hand, rural enterprises could improve technology by cooperating with research institutes and universities.

Some rural enterprises in coastal areas had also started to cooperate with foreign businesses through equity and contractual joint-ventures and other arrangements with overseas Chinese and foreign businesses so that rural enterprises could buy advanced equipment, technologies, craftsmanship, and management skills. For example, Jiangkou town, Putia County, Fujian utilized funds invested by overseas Chinese to import advanced technologies and

119

equipment, and through various joint operation arrangements, it had put its products on the world market. By 1987, there were 1,159 large and small enterprises in the township (Xu Yu, 1987, pp.16-20).

In short, cooperation in technology between state enterprises and rural enterprises, between research institutes or universities and rural enterprises and between foreign businesses and rural enterprises had helped in promoting technological development of rural enterprises as well as improving production in rural enterprises. Nevertheless, the extent of technological collaboration on a national level remained relatively poor. The 'haves' were unwilling to provide advanced technology to the 'have-nots' instead preferring to maintain their advantage over potential competitors. The level of technology being transferred to rural enterprises was typically out-of-date productive capacity discarded by enterprises after they had upgraded their own facilities. The poor level of technological development in the countryside thus remained an important obstacle to growth in this area, and to the establishment of a more efficient rural industrial sector.

Conclusion

From 1978 to 1992, the Chinese government had emphasized the need to improve the technological level of rural enterprises. This policy and its implementation had important implications for technological progress in rural enterprises. The Spark Plan played a positive role in promoting relatively large-scale rural enterprises. The increase in the mobility of technological personnel between research institutes and rural enterprises not only helped to exploit the potential of scarce technological and professional manpower, but also to an extent helped to solve the shortage of technological personnel in rural enterprises. Cooperation in technology played a very important role in promoting the technological development of rural enterprises.

However, although China's government had taken some measures to improve the technology in rural enterprises, some problems such as the shortages of technological personnel and finance, low educational level of workers still remained. In addition, obsolete facilities, outdated techniques, and the shortage of qualified personnel, were the major obstacles to improve the quality of products, and reduce raw material consumption.

Moreover, rural enterprises were facing new difficulties. Rural enterprises had gradually lost their privileges under the new situation brought on by reforms. The concessionary tax and credit policies originally enjoyed had been gradually cancelled. The means of production had seen great price rises. Therefore, many rural enterprises realized that they had to rely on technological progress to increase competitiveness and adaptability.

9 Conclusion

Positive roles of public policy changes for rural enterprises

When the reformist leadership of Deng Xiaoping assumed power in December 1978, the CCP was facing a crisis of legitimacy. Although there were serious disagreements among the new leadership over the best way forward for China, a consensus developed among the party leadership that policy changes had to occur if the Party was to retain its position and the country was not to slide further behind its competitors in terms of economic development. As Carol Hamrin (1989, p.116) wrote: 'From the beginning, Deng Xiaoping viewed the economic reform program not only as a necessity for national well being, but also as a survival kit for the CCP'. It is therefore impossible to separate the economic and political imperatives behind policy changes towards rural enterprises after 1978 - the survival of the CCP was perceived as being dependent on the rapid development of the Chinese economy.

This study has demonstrated that changes in public policy from 1978 to 1992 did play positive roles in promoting the development of rural enterprises. These positive roles had been manifested in the following areas. First, and of crucial importance, the ideological base of policy had changed from one of restraining the development of collective rural enterprises before 1978 to encouraging the development of rural enterprises after 1978. Perhaps the most dramatic change occurred in the official attitude towards the private sector of rural enterprises. From being prohibited during the Maoist era, the private sector of rural enterprises was not only tolerated after 1978, but in the case of Wenzhou, had been actively encouraged and promoted as a positive model by some Chinese leaders. Without these fundamental changes of policy, political climate would not have been conducive to the development of rural enterprises.

Secondly, the extension of more decision making powers to local governments allowed local governments considerable leeway in formulating policies to aid the development of rural enterprises. As a result, different development approaches had emerged in different areas depending on local regional economic and geographical conditions. As demonstrated in Chapter Three, development strategies in Wenzhou were fundamentally different from those adopted in Wuxi. As a result, it is not possible to talk in terms of a single development model for rural enterprises. There were large disparities in the scope and nature of developments across China as a whole. These disparities had not only been affected by local development strategies, but had also been influenced by the uneven development programme adopted in the 1980s. In combination, these policy changes had resulted in wide divergences in development, not only between the three large regions (west, centre and coast) but also within regions.

Thirdly, the expansion of market mechanisms as a means to regulate the economy had facilitated the development of rural enterprises. Freed from the constraints of bureaucratic management and allocation of resources, rural enterprises were able to buy more raw materials and get more funds in free markets. Without this development, the expansion of rural enterprises would have been strictly limited.

However, although the introduction of market mechanisms had undoubtedly facilitated the development of rural enterprises, the change from the old system had not been total. The hand of bureaucratic management was still very visible, particularly in the state run sector. With many products in short supply on the domestic market, the government had frequently intervened to ensure the provision of adequate supplies to large scale state owned enterprises deemed to be essential components of the national economy. In these situations, rural enterprises became squeezed by the government's commitment to the state sector, and found it difficult to gain access to essential raw materials. In essence, when times were good, rural enterprises benefited from the development of the market, but when times got hard, they found themselves at the bottom of the government's pecking order for the allocation of resources. Like most sectors of the Chinese economy, rural enterprises had faced difficulties due to the partial nature of reform. However on balance, I must conclude that even the partial introduction of the market had been more conducive to the development of rural enterprises than no market at all.

Fourthly, in order to solve the problem of huge numbers of rural surplus labourers in rural areas, the government had adopted the development of rural enterprises as the most important strategy in solving rural unemployment since 1978. The government had remained in tight control of peasants' rights to migrate to big cities, but it had adopted a more liberal policy to allow peasants to establish rural enterprises in small towns. This provided a strong incentive for farmers to develop rural enterprises.

Fifthly, the government had provided collective rural enterprises with preferential treatment in terms of bank credit and tax rates, although state loans towards rural enterprises had decreased since late 1988 and tax burdens on rural enterprises gradually increased. Since 1978, the increase of peasant incomes had enabled rural enterprises to raise funds from individuals and society in various ways. Therefore, government financial and tax policies had created more favourable financial conditions for developing rural enterprises.

Sixthly, the government had provided some policies to improve management in rural enterprises, especially in township or village owned enterprises. The government had implemented the contractual responsibility system and a responsibility system for factory directors. The government also changed the payment system for labour and adopted a policy to promote the quality of production in rural enterprises. As a result, these policies had played a positive role in improving management in rural enterprises.

Seventhly, since 1978 the technological strategy of the government had been changed from an emphasis on small scale labour intensive methods of production to the use of appropriate technology. The reform of the science and technology management system had given rural enterprises more opportunities to obtain advanced technology. The government had also taken some practical measures to promote technology in rural enterprises, including the implementation of the 'Spark Plan' and the policy to allow technological personnel to work in rural enterprises in their spare time and the promotion of cooperation in technology between state enterprises and rural enterprises and between research institutes and universities and rural enterprises. These measures had also promoted technology in rural enterprises.

Economic and political problems for the development of rural enterprises

The changes outlined above had combined to create an economic and political environment that had facilitated the development of rural enterprises. But despite these advances, the change of public policy had been inadequate. On the

124

long march to the situation where rural enterprises can play a full and valuable role in the Chinese economy, there is still a long way to go.

Although private enterprises had acquired a legal status, private enterprises still faced many difficulties and different forms of discrimination. Similarly, there was still considerable discrimination against rural enterprises (whether they are collective run or private run enterprises) particularly in the supply of raw materials and credits, compared with the policy towards state enterprises.

Since 1978, the reform of the market had created a more favourable market environment for the development of rural enterprises. However, rural enterprises had not enjoyed the same competitive position as state enterprise in many areas such as product transport, retailing and export. With the further reform of the economic system in the cities, the large and medium state enterprises had taken further steps to relax restrictions in order to invigorate their operations. At the same time, however, some privileges of state enterprises remained. In addition, with the increase in the level of wages and benefits for staff workers, the cost of labour in rural areas had increased. With the gradual opening of the market, the prices of energy and raw materials had continued to rise, so that rural enterprises had paid higher costs. With the intensification of competition in the market, increasingly higher demands had also been made of rural enterprises in the technical standard and quality of their products. Thus, situations where rural enterprises enjoyed a position of superiority, normally or abnormally, had already, and I would argue prematurely, begun to fade away. In addition, the preferential treatments in credit and taxes formerly accorded rural enterprises had gradually been reduced.

If the benefits of the introduction of market mechanisms had been tempered, so the devolution of powers to local authorities had been a double edged sword. The shortage of fiscal income in local communities and local government funds for welfare work and agricultural funds had led to the problem of local government exacting a large percentage of profit, and collecting excessive charges. Although the central government had implemented a policy of reducing the financial burden of rural enterprises, some problems such as exacting a large percentage of profits, collecting excessive charges, and allowing rural enterprises to retain only a small percentage of profits had remained.

Government policies to promote technology in rural enterprises had also been inadequate. The shortage of technological personnel and finance and the low educational level of workers remained formidable obstacles for the progress of technology in rural enterprises.

Moreover, some political and ideological questions had remained an obstacle restraining rural enterprises' ability to make even greater progress. One

125

complaint against rural enterprises had been that the development of rural enterprises affected agricultural production.

The rapid development of rural enterprises had widened the discrepancy between the income of rural enterprise workers and peasants; hence, a problem involving agricultural production had arisen. According to a study conducted in Southern Jiangsu Province, peasants were unwilling to stop planting grain, but they were also unwilling to plant too much. They did not want to stop planting because their past experience of hunger urged them not to abandon grain production. They did not want to plant too much because the economic results of land cultivation was about 30 per cent lower than that of industrial work (Chou Yuan and Chao Ming, 1985, p.24). This had caused considerable waste of farmland. In addition, large tracts of farmland had been occupied by flourishing rural enterprises. These two factors had contributed to a sharp decrease in farmland in these years.

However, the problems of agriculture should not be blamed entirely on the development of rural enterprises. On the contrary, rural enterprises had supported the development of agriculture with large amounts of funds. For example, in 1989, Zhejiang and Shanghai on average received 200 to 300 yuan per person per year in 'supplementing agriculture' money (Su Bei, 1989, pp.32-34). This suggests that the view that rural enterprises had caused the agricultural decline was unjustified.

Another complaint against rural enterprises had been that rural enterprises had polluted the environment. A study was published in 1988 by environmentalists and ecologists from the Chinese scientific and other research institutions (CD, 13 October 1988), which pointed out that the most flourishing rural industries were built without any consideration for the environment since 1978. In a report on environmental problems caused by China's small town and village industries, the scientists predicted that if rural enterprises continue to increase at a 25 to 30 per cent growth rate, their industrial waste water will account for 40 to 50 per cent of the country's total by the year 2,000. A test of the atmosphere in seven provinces where 12,000 rural enterprises were located shows that the content of toxicant elements in the air, such as benzene, silicon dust and asbestos, surpassed the standards set forth by the state public health authorities by several hundred or even one thousand times (CD, 13 October 1988). The waste water coming from rural industries accounted for only 10 per cent of the country's total industrial waste water release, but in some highly-developed areas such as Southern Jiangsu Province, industrial population in surrounding rural townships had been large-scale. Moreover, areas specializing in the production of sulphur, coke, bricks and tiles had serious effects on the atmosphere, though large-scale

126

air pollution had not been detected (*CD*, 13 October 1988). Thus, environmental problems should be considered when rural enterprises are established. China's environmental protection policies should in future pay greater attention to rural ecological environment even though its priority may remain focused on urban areas.

Private enterprises were only officially legalized in 1988, and had traditionally been considered 'capitalist ownership'. As a result, political and ideological problems for private enterprises had been more severe. Some local party leaders had expressed concern that the existence and development of private enterprises might lead to private entrepreneurs becoming a distinct class infiltrating the state sector. This could result in the 'restoration of capitalism', which would change the face of socialism and the nature of society in China (*LW*, 1988, pp.12-14). However, whether the economic reform policies would bring about fundamental changes in the political system would depend largely on whether the private sector of the economy could become strong enough to account for a significant part of China's GNP. The output value of the private economy still only accounted for a very low percentage of the gross output value of Chinese industry. Nonetheless, the newly risen entrepreneurs with their increased wealth and social influence had brought demands for political influence and social standing.

It was reported that more than 200,000 members of the CCP engaged in the private sector of the economy in early 1989 (*DGB*, 16 March 1989). This means that on average one out of 235 members of the CCP was involved in the private sector of economy in early 1989. Among the entrepreneurs in the survey of private rural enterprises (*NYJJWT*, No.2, 1989, pp.18-23), 21.6 per cent were members of the Communist Party of China, 6.2 per cent were members of the Communist Youth League of China, 8.2 per cent held positions in Village CCP Committees and Village Committees, 15.5 per cent had relatives who worked in the government of the town (township) or county, or other public organizations. This data suggested that entrepreneurs had certain influence in rural areas. It also suggested that party membership, or links with party members, could ease the process of establishing and running private enterprises. The popular suspicion that private enterprises went hand in hand with corruption had not been eased by such a relationship. Thus, it could be said that the private economy had already played a considerable role in Chinese politics.

Furthermore, the working conditions for employees in enterprises owned by party members was not in accord with the party constitution, which called for its members to make concerted efforts to eliminate exploitation in China. It was argued that if these members would not have used all their income from

127

exploitation for investment, the improvement of people's well-being and Party members dues, or if their enterprises would not be transformed into collective enterprises, these members should be asked to quit the Party (*CD*, 30 April 1988). Although these employment practices had been justified as a means to achieve common prosperity and the development of a commodity economy, this did confuse the ideology of the members of the CCP. With the development of private enterprises in China, criticisms of the connection between party membership and private ownership of enterprises had continued to be expressed.

As noted above, the main public complaint against private enterprises had been in terms of corruption and illegal practices. As I have demonstrated in Chapter Six, large numbers of rural enterprises had been guilty of tax evasion. In addition, the highly monopolized financial organizations had made it very hard for private enterprises to obtain loans, which sometimes were only available with 'good personal connections'. Thus private businesses had been forced to depend on favours and gifts in order to obtain raw materials, sell their goods and raise loans. It could therefore be argued that any corruption that arises was the fault of the partial nature of reform, which allowed private enterprises to legally exist, but did not allow them to get what they physically needed to exist. Nevertheless, in the eyes of much of the population, corruption was still being blamed on the existence of private enterprises, and not the economic system that they were forced to exist in.

The development of private enterprises had widened disparities between the rich and the poor and between different regions. The result had been an increase in social tension. For example, in a survey of 100 private rural enterprises, the average initial capital of each enterprise was 32,000 yuan. After three to four years, the average capital of each enterprise reached 144,000 yuan (*NYJJWT*, No.2, 1989, p.19). Furthermore, most private enterprises operated in more developed rural areas along the coast (*CD*, 15 April 1988). By contrast, some areas hindered by poor geographical conditions, conservative views, and a low level of education, had not solved problems of poverty and backwardness. In addition, some entrepreneurs had articulated the fear that government officials might find ways to reorganize their businesses in the future. Thus, wealthy entrepreneurs in some areas had hit on the idea of making gifts of money, and providing other favours to cadres in the hopes of averting future problems (*LW*, 25 January 1988, No.4, pp.7-9).

In the past, China condemned the capitalist theory. However, since 1978 it had admitted that a private economy in China could promote production, provided employment opportunities, and helped in many other ways to meet people's needs. Thus, traditional Marxist-Leninist ideology could not guide present policy. Some theoreticians had tried to find new theories to explain the problem of the emergence of new economic and social forces. They argued that China must comprehensively and correctly reassess modern capitalism - especially capitalism since World War II - and called for the assimilation of the positive aspects and achievements of capitalism.

Meanwhile, however, the development and existence of the private sector had brought it into competition with public ownership of the economic system. On the one hand, this competition could improve the administration and management of public ownership, as well as raising the quality of services within the state and collective systems. On the other hand, the very rapid development of private enterprises had caused state run businesses severe difficulties. Thus, the superiority of state ownership had been brought into doubt.

For example, Wenzhou had a proportionately bigger private economy than anywhere else in China. In Wenzhou, state run businesses which were managed over the past thirty years had been surpassed by private companies which had developed in a mere three to five years. Traditional management ideas and methods used by state run businesses had been decimated by furious competition and were left no choice but to undergo whole scale revision. Three Chinese scholars at the Chinese Academy of Social Sciences made the strongest case for a reform policy based on attacking state ownership and gave a plan for 'privatising China' (*TE*, 11 February 1989, Vol.310, p.70). After the events of 4 June 1989, the plan of privatising China had officially been denied (Jin Qi, 1989). Although this proposal was rejected by the Chinese government, the proportion of public ownership has continued to fall. Private enterprises were among the hardest hit during the national austerity programme implemented between 1988 and 1991. According to the State Administration of Industry and Commerce, more than 1 million self-employed people across the country went out of business in the first few months of 1989. Not only were many existing private businesses closing, but the number of new self-employed households registering was also declining (Wen Jia, 1989). The main reason behind the decrease was that of the state's rectification of private businesses (*BR*, 6-12 November 1989).

Another reason for the decline was the impact of the austerity programmes launched in September 1988. According to Wang Zhongming, director of the administration's individual and private economy department, these programs decreased the amount of bank loans, raw materials, fuel and other resources available to private businesses. For example, in Wenzhou, local banks did not allow individual businessmen to withdraw money, resulting in about 300,000

129

businessmen and their partners reaching the verge of bankruptcy (Chen Xiao, 3 January 1989). Other factors included poor management, indiscriminate fines and fees, extortion and fund shortages. Therefore, although the legal status of private enterprises changed in the 1980s, many problems remained. The crucial factor had been the continued existence of a political and ideological environment that fostered suspicion (and even downright hostility) to the private sector.

However, although some economic and political problems remained, China's leaders were aware that farmers cannot rely on the limited arable land to improve their living standards and solve rural unemployment. Moreover, agricultural modernization and the improvement of rural communication and transport services also depend on the development of rural enterprises since the government cannot invest much money for agriculture when poorly run state owned industries, regarded as the backbone of the national economy, constantly need more money themselves.

Even during the austerity programme of late 1988 to 1991, new policies affecting rural enterprises were still formulated. In 1990, for example, the 'Regulations for Collective Rural Enterprises in the PRC' was passed. The 'Decision of the CCP Central Committee on Further Strengthening Agriculture and the Work in Rural Areas', adopted by the eighth plenary session of the 13th CCP Central Committee on 29th November 1991, also indicated that actively developing township and town enterprises was considered to be the way to develop the rural economy, and to increase peasants' income, and to speed up agricultural modernization and national economic development (*SWB/FE*, 3 January 1992). The decision further called for the giving of active support to township and town enterprises.

Irrespective of whether China's leaders like rural enterprises or not, they can no longer overlook the economic strength of rural enterprises. Most of them expressed their support for rural enterprises. Deng Xiaoping highly praised these enterprises as a new force that had suddenly come to the fore because of rural reform (*ZGXZQYB*, 13 February 1991). Party secretary general Jiang Zemin had similarly stated that the role of rural enterprises not only lay in having industry nourish both agricultural and sideline production, but also lay in close ties with urban large-scale industry and foreign trade, as well as close ties with agricultural and nonstaple food production (*ZGXZQYB*, 13 February 1991). The current prime minister, Li Peng, stated that: 'In my opinion, we should correctly assess the role that can be played by town and village enterprises in developing China's economy' (*QS*, No.6, 16 March 1990, pp.6-9).

In the past several years, China's government has continued to implement some policies promoting the development of rural enterprises, especially in central and western regions, and rural enterprises have continued to develop dramatically. Therefore, it is reasonably certain that the Chinese government will continue to permit, and even encourage the development of rural enterprises.

Implications for the former communist countries and developing countries

Since the majority of China's rural enterprises are small scale enterprises, China's experience of the development of rural enterprises has important implications for the development of small-scale enterprises in many former communist countries and developing countries. This study has shown that the main stimulus for the extraordinary growth of China's rural enterprises from 1978 to 1992 had been the removal of restrictions, although policy changes toward rural enterprises, like that in many other fields of economic reforms, had by no means been wholly *laissez-faire*. The extraordinary growth of rural enterprises had contributed immensely to the improvement of living standards in China's rural areas and the creation of rural employment, but also helped maintain political stability of rural areas. Although more and more countries have realized the importance of small-scale enterprises, there are still many places where the policy environment for small scale enterprises is still fiercely repressive, or others where there is effectively no policy at all. Policy makers in these places can certainly learn from China's experience and make favourable policy changes so that small scale enterprises can be freed from the different policy restrictions.

China's experience has shown that the attitude of local governments is a very important determinant of success or failure of small scale enterprises. If local officers have the strong motive to support the development of small scale enterprises, they may even create their own policies outside the framework of central government policies. It would be a good idea for the promotion and rewards of local officers to be linked to the development of small scale enterprises so that local officers have the incentive to promote the development of small scale enterprises.

The entrepreneurs of small scale enterprises in many countries can also learn from the experience of China's rural entrepreneurs how to survive and even prosper in an extraordinarily difficult policy environment. As I have discussed in the above chapters, China's rural entrepreneurs adopted the different

131

strategies to deal with restricted central policies. For example, when central policy prohibited the development of private rural enterprises, they borrowed 'red hat' from township and village owned enterprises to register as 'collective' enterprises so that they could survive and develop. When central government tightened financial policy, they raised funds by themselves. As a result, they had survived and even prospered in such a difficult policy environment.

The foregoing study has shown that appropriate government sponsored assistance programmes can bring positive results. However, these assistance programmes can only reach a small minority of rural enterprises. Liberal policies towards the issues such as product specifications, or any similar aspects of industrial undertakings are very important. Although China's government had laid down a guideline to improve product quality, enforcement had been weak since local officers gave greater weight to jobs and growth than to product quality and other standards. Malcolm Harper wrote:

> They remain in force and are an obvious pretext for petty corruption since any policeman or similar official can be fairly sure of finding some regulation which a given firm is breaking. Compliance is quite beyond their reach, but a small 'tip' buys a blind eye until the next official is in need of ready cash (Harper, Malcolm, 1984, p.37).

Small businesses in many developing countries find it quite impossible to obey many strict standards which come from industrialised countries. Liberal policies towards the issues such as product specifications, or any similar aspects of industrial undertakings would no doubt benefit the development of small scale enterprises.

Bibliography

American Rural Small-Scale Industry Delegation. (1977), *Rural Small-Scale Industry in the People's Republic of China*, Berkeley: University of California Press.

Andors, Stephen.(1977), *China's Industrial Revolution--Politics, Planning, and Management, 1949 to the Present*, Martin Robertson & Co. Ltd, London.

Anderson, Dennis and Khambata, Farida. (1981), *Small Enterprises and Development Policy in the Philippines: A Case Study*, World Bank Staff Working Papers, No. 468.

Ash, Robert F. (1988), 'The Evolution of Agricultural Policy', *CQ*, December, pp.529-555.

Bao Weihe. (1986), 'Suggestions on Profit Distribution Reform of Township and Enterprises', *NYKJYJ*, No.2, pp.20-22.

Bao Weihuo. (1986), 'Variety of Wage System for Diverse Small-scale Enterprises', *NCCWKJ*, No. 7, pp.26-28.

Bao Youti. (1990), 'A Symposium Summary--Views on Township Enterprises in the Eighth Five-Plan and in the 10-Year Development Plan', *ZGNCJJ*, No.8, pp.62-64.

Bi Guohua and Bao Yonghong. (1989), 'An Analytical Report of the Questionnaire Data on Macro-Management of Township and Town Enterprises', *NYJJ*, Liaoning, No.3.

BR. (27 December 1982), 'Constitution of the People's Republic of China', Vol.25, No.52, pp.10-29.

BR. (21 May 1984), 'Small Towns and Rural Markets in China', Vol.27, No.21, p.25.

BR. (8-14 February 1988), 'Zhao on Coastal Areas' Development Strategy', Vol.31, No.6, pp.14-19.

BR. (27 February - 5 March 1989), 'Going It Alone - An Account of Private Entrepreneur', Vol. 32, No.9, pp.19-22.

BR. (7-13 August 1989), 'Strengthening Taxation's Role as an Economic Lever', Vol.32, No.32, pp.16-19.

BR. (2-8 October 1989), 'Top Party Leaders Answer Questions at Press Conference', *BR*, Vol.32, No.40, pp.15-18.

BR. (6-12 November 1989), 'Private Businesses Need Protection', Nol.32, No.45, pp.7-8.

BR. (22-28 January 1990), 'Rural Firms to Face Period of Austerity', Vol.33, No.4, pp.28-29.

BR. (28 May - 3 June 1990), 'Integrating Planned Economy With Market Regulation', Vol.33, No.22, pp.16-18.

BR. (17-23 December 1990), 'Facts and Figures: Geographical Distribution, Density and National Growth Rate of China's Population', Vol.33, No.51, pp.21-23.

BR. (15-21 June 1992), 'Deng the Whirlwind Rejuvenates Wenzhou', Vol.35, No.24, pp.4-5.

Breslin, Shaun. (1995), *China in the 1980s: Centre-Province Relations in a Reforming Socialist State* , Macmillion.

Byrd, William A. (1990), 'Entrepreneurship, Capital, and Ownership', in William A.Byrd and Lin Qingsong. (eds), *China's Rural Industry--Structure, Development, and Reform*, Oxford University Press.

Byrd, William A. and Gelb, Alan. (1990), 'Why Industrialize? The Incentive for Rural Community Governments', in William A.Byrd and Lin Qingsong. (eds), *China's Rural Industry--Structure, Development, and Reform*, Oxford University Press, pp.342-357.

CD. (6 February 1986), 'Rural Area Industries Face Growth Challenge'.

CD. (6 June 1987), 'Rural Industry Helps Agriculture'.

CD. (3 November 1987), 'Rural Industry Needs Experts'.

CD. (12 November 1987), 'Materials Market Sets an Example'.

CD. (14 December 1987), 'Family-Run Enterprises Prosper'.

CD. (15 December 1987), 'Policy Encourages Individual Sector'.

CD. (16 December 1987), 'Township Enterprises Take Aim at World'.

CD. (19 December 1987), 'Zhao Calls Rural Firms One of Keys to Exports'.

CD. (26 March 1988), 'Township Enterprises Catch Up'.

CD. (15 April 1988), 'Law to Guarantee Role of Private Sector'.

CD. (22 April 1988), 'Problems Exist in Private Firms'.

CD. (30 April 1988), 'Opposite Views on Private Business'.

CD. (26 May 1988), 'Private High-tech Companies Progress'.

CD. (27 May 1988), 'Private Businesses Face Many Difficulties'.

CD. (20 July 1988), 'Exports Suit Rural Industries'.

CD. (6 October 1988), ''Double Track' Price Stir Debate'.

CD. (13 October 1988), 'Polluting Industries Endanger Rural Areas'.

CD. (2 November 1988), 'Market System Promoted'.

CD. (17 February 1992), 'Rural firms Seen as Solution to Many Problems'.

CD. (25 February 1992), 'Rural Industry Gives Boost to Nation's Economy'.

Chen Qingzhong. (1986), 'Bright Prospects in Township Industry Investment', *JJYFL*, Vol 5, Hong Kong, pp.10-11.

Chen Tesheng. (1986), 'The Development of Town and Township Enterprises in Mainland China Since 1979', *IS*, Vol. 22, No.10.

Chen Xiao. (1989), 'Private Businesses Have Bright Future', *CD*, 3 January.

Cheng Chu-yuan. (1982), *China's Economic Development--Growth and Structural Change*, Westview Press, Boulder, Colorado.

Chou Yuan and Chao Ming. (1985), 'Agriculture in Southern Jiangsu After the Development of Township and Town Enterprises', *LW*, No.29.

Christiansen, Flemming. (1989), 'The Justification and Legalization of Private Enterprises in China, 1983-1988', *CI*, Volume IV, No.2, pp.78-91.

Chuang Meng. (1992), 'Deng's Struggle against Leftist; and Why Zhao Ziyang Has White Hair', *Jing Bao* (Jing Journal), Hong Kong, 5 January.

David, Paul A. (1975), *Technical Choice Innovation and Economic growth*, Cambridge University Press.

Delfs, Robert. (1990), 'China Seeks Ways to End Local Protectionism-Beggar the Neighbour', *FEER*, 18 October.

Du Haiyan. (1988), 'Analysis of China's Town and Township Enterprise Administrative System', *ZGNCJJ*, No.6, pp.21-32.

Du Haiyan. (1990), 'Causes of Rapid Rural Industrial Development', in William A. Byrd and Lin Qingsong. (eds), *China's Rural Industry Structure, Development, and Reform*, Oxford University Press, pp.47-62.

Enos, J.E. (1984), 'Commune and Brigade Run Industries in Rural China: Some Recent Obervational Reform and Economic Development in the Chinese Countryside,' in Keith Griffin. (eds), *Institutional Reform and Economic Development in the Chinese Countryside*, London, Macmillan Press, pp.223-252.

Feng Lanrui and Jiang Weiyu. (1988), 'A Comparative Study of the Modes of Transference of Surplus Labour in China's Countryside', *SSIC*, Beijing, September, pp.64-77.

Fei Xiaotong. (1985a), 'China's Road to Rural Industrialization', *BR*, Vol.28, No.14, 8 April, pp.24-26.

Fei Xiaotong. (1985b), 'Rural, Urban Industries Melded Together', *BR*, Vol.28, No.17, 29 April, pp. 22-23.

Feng, C.L. (1988), 'Here Agricuture, Industry Work Side-By-Side', *CD*, 10 February.

Forster, K. (1990), *Rebellion and Factionalism in a Chinese Province: Zhejiang, 1966-1976* , New York: M. E. Sharpe.

Gao Jinan. (1988), 'Unions Will Be Set Up in Private Firms Soon', *CD*, 24 November.

Gao Jinian. (1988), 'City's Private Firms Get Hiring Permits', *CD*, November 7.

Gelb, A. (1990), 'TVP Workers' Incomes, Incentives, and Attitudes', in edited by Byrd, William A. and Lin Qingsong, *China's Rural Industry--Structure, Development, and Reform*, Oxford University Press, pp.280-298.

Gelb, A. and Svejnar, J. (1990), 'Chinese TVPs in an International Perspective', in Byrd, William A. and Lin Qingsong. (eds), *China's Rural Industry-- Structure, Development, and Reform*, Oxford University Press, pp.342-357.

Gray, Jack. (1982), 'Rural enterprises in China 1977-79', in Jack Grary and G.White (eds), *China's New Development Strategy*, Academic Press, New York, pp.211-233.

Griffin, Keith and Griffin, Kimberley. (1984), 'Commune-and Brigade- run Enterprises in Rural China: An Overview', in Griffin, Keith. (eds), *Institutional reform and Economic Development in the Chinese Countryside*, Macmillan Press, pp.210-222.

Gu Chengwen.(1988), 'Private Businesses Create Millionaires', *CD*, 5 December.

Gu Chengwen. (1989), 'Jiangsu to Shut Down Pooly-run Rural Firms', *CD*, 25 March.

Gu Tiefeng. (1986), 'Theories Concerning the Implementation of the Shares System Need Further Exploration-Discussion on Theory and Practice of an Enterprise Shares System', Beijing, *JJCK*, 4 June.

Guo Yanquan. (1986), 'The Trend of a Drastic Decrease in Farmland in Our Country Deserves Close Attention', Beijing, *JJZB*, 22 June.

Guo Zhongshi. (1987), 'Success of Small Towns Matches the Big Cites', *CD*, 11 November.

Hamrin, Carol. (1989), *China and the Challenge of the Future*, Westwiew Press.

Han Baocheng. (1987), 'Industry Becomes Important in Countryside', *BR*, Vol.30, No.23, 8 June, pp.20-23.

Han Baocheng. (1988), 'Importance Attached to Coastal Development', *BR*, 25 April 25- 1 May, Vol.31, No.17, pp.16-17.

Han Baocheng. (1990), 'Readjustment Improves Rural Enterprises', *BR*, Vol.33, No.35, 27 August - 2 September, pp.13-21.

Han Zhiguo. (1986), 'Trends in the Development of the Private Economy and How to Deal with Them - Summary of Forum on the Development of the Private Economy in Our Country', *JJRB*, 8 November.

Han Zhiguo. (1986), 'The Labour Force Remains a Commodity Under Socialist Conditions -- A Discussion on the Ideas of Comrades Wang Jue and Xiao Xin', *GMRB*, 2 August and 16 August.

Harper, Malcolm and Tan Thiam Soon (1979), *Small Enterprises in Developing Countries: Case Studies and Conclusions*, Intermediate Technology Publications Ltd, London.

Harper, Malcolm (1984), 'The Policy Environment', in Harper, Malcolm (ed.), *Small Business in The Third World: Guidelines for Practical Assistance*, Intermediate Technology Publications Ltd, London, pp.36-44.

He Jiazheng. (1987), 'The Magic and Charm of the Market - General Trend of Economic Changes in China's Rural Areas', *RMRB*, 20 November.

He Kuang (1984), 'How Can the Superiority of Socialism Be Brought into Play Discussion of Economic Structural Reform', *RMRB*, 25 October.

Ho, Samuel P.S. (1986), *The Asian Experience in Rural Nonagricultural Development and Its Relevance for China*, The World Bank Staff Working Papers Number 757.

Hoselitz, B.F. (1959), 'Small Industry in Underdeveloped Countries', *Journal of Economic History*, Vol. 19.

Hogwood, Brian W. and Gunn, Lewis A. (1984), 'Policy Analysis for the Real World', Oxford University Press.

Hsu R. (1992), *Economic Theories in China, 1979-1988* , Cambridge and New York: Cambridge University Press.

Huang Shouhong. (1990a), 'Town and Township Enterprises as a Motive Force in the Development of the National Economy', *JJYJ*, No.5, pp.39-46.

Huang Shouhong. (1990b), 'Exports of Township Enterprises in Eastern China Are Brisk', *JFRB*, 18 October.

Hu Yinkang. (1985), 'The reform of Household Registration Regulations and the Needs of Economic Development', *Shehui Kexue* (Social Sciences), No.6.

Huang Xu. (1987), 'What Is the Southern Jiangsu Model, and What Is the 'Wenzhou Model?' *XXYYJ*, 5 January, pp.37-38.

Jin Qi. (1989), 'Why China Will Not Practise Privatization', *BR*, Vol.32, No.36, 4-10 September, pp.4-5.

JJRB. (31 July 1986), 'The Universal Significance of the 'Wenzhou Pattern''.

Jones, Peter. (1992), 'Evaluation', in Harrop, Martin. (ed.), *Power and Policy in Liberal Democracies*, Cambridge University Press, pp.241-262.

Kaplan, Fredric M. (ed.).(1979), *Encyclopedia of China Today*, The Macmillan Press Ltd.

Ke Bingsheng. (1990), 'Regional Differences in China's Rural Enterprise Development and Their Causes', *NYJJWT*, No 10, 23 October, pp.33-36.

Kolb, Eugene J. (1978), *A Framework for Political Analysis*, Prictice Hall, USA.

Krongkaew, Medhi. (1988), 'The Development of Small and Medium-Scale Industries in Thailand', *ADB*, Vol.6, No.2, pp.70-95.

Ku Sungnien and Yen Yinglung. (1985), 'The Study of Economic Theories Involving Township and Town Enterprises Is Being Advanced in Practice', *JJYJ*, No.5.

Lardy, Nicholas R. (1983), *Agriculture in China's Modern Economic Development*, Cambridge University Press.

Lei Xilu. (1986), 'Diversified Economy Attracts Surplus Labourers', *BR*, No.47, 24 November, pp.16-18.

Li Qingzeng. (1986), 'A Discussion of the Problems of Rural Surplus Labour', *NYJJWT*, No.10, pp.8-11.

Li Shih-chun. (1987), 'Township Enterprises and the Production of Consumer Goods', Hong Kong, *Jingji Daobao*(Economic Herald), No.47, 30 November.

Li Shihui. (1987), 'On the Patterns of Rural Surplus Labours Transfer and Different Theoretical Opinions', *NYJJWT*, No.1 1987, pp.49-53.

Li Shuzhong. (1987), 'Preliminary Impact of Spark Plan on Chinese Agriculture', Hong Kong, *LW*, Overseas Edition, No.12, pp.14-16.

Li Yongzeng. (1986), 'The Fast Developing Individual Economy in China', *LW*, Overseas Edition, No.50, pp. 21-22.

Li Wei. (1988), 'Finding Oneself in a Storm', *JJRB*, 24 August.

Lin Qingsong. (1990), 'Private Enterprise: Their Emergence, Rapid Growth, and Problems' in William A. Byrd and Lin Qingsong. (eds), *China's Rural Industry--Structure, Development, and Reform*, Oxford University Press, pp.172-188.

Lin Zilin. (1986), 'A Report on Commodity Economy and Labour Hiring Problems in Wenzhou', *JJZB*, 9 November.

Ling Zhijun. (1986), 'Where the Potential Lies -- Commenting on the Emerging Individually Operated Rural Enterprises', *RMRB*, 29 November.

Little, I.M.D. (1988), 'Small Manufacturing Enterprises and Employment in Developing Countries', *ADB*, Vol.6, No.2, pp.1-9.

Liu, A. (1992), 'The Wenzhou Model of Development and China's Modernization', *AS*, No. 8, pp. 696-697.

Liu Guoguang. (1985), 'Tentative Discussion on the Transformation of the Two Economic Patterns in Our Country on Economic Reform and Control: Linking Planning and the Market', *RMRB*, 4 November.

Liu Guoguang. (1987), 'Unifying Planning and Marketing', *BR*, Vol.30, No.41, 12 October.

Liu Guoguang and Zhao Renwei. (1982), 'Relationship Between Planning and the Market Under Socialism', in George C.Wang. (edited and translated), *Economic Reform in the PRC*, pp.89-104.

Liu Guoguan. (1989), 'A Sweet and Sour Decade', *BR*, 2-8 January, pp.22-29.

Liu Shiqiang. (1985), 'Opportunities and New Challenges Facing Small Town Enterprises in the Course of Development', *Kunming Jingji Wenti Tansuo* (Kunming Economic Problem Research), No.9, pp.29-32.

Liu Xiaojing. (1988), 'Some Issues in the Healthy Development of Private Enterprises: An Empirical Analysis of 130 Private Enterprises in 18 Provinces', *NYJJWT*, No.4, 1988.

Liu Yia-ling. (1992), 'Reform From Below: The Private Economy and Local Politics, No.130, *CQ*, pp.293-316.

Liu Wenpu. (1988), 'Privatization of Collective Enterprises in Rural Areas', *ZGNCJJ*, No.10, pp 27-32.

Liu Zhihong. (1986), 'On Fundraising for Town and Township Enterprises', *NYKJYJ*, Beijing, No.3, pp.48-50.

Liu Zhongkui. (1986), 'Town and township Enterprises and 'Spark Plan'', Tianjin, *Jishu Shichang Bao*(Technological Market Daily), 4 February, pp.1-3.

Lu Shenliang. (1986), 'A Look at Economic Growth in Wenzhou', *RMRB*, Overseas Edition, 29 May.

Lu Tianrong. (1987), 'Industries Help Develop Rural Areas', *CD*, 10 October.

Lu Xueyi. (1986), 'The Development of Township and Town Enterprises Is Key to the Second Step in Rural Reform', *JJRB*, Beijing, 18 October, p.1.

Lu Yan. (1987), 'Contract Disputes by Individually Owned Small Businesses', *WGYZL*, 5 January, pp. 27-28.

Lu Yun. (1984), 'Rural Township Enterprises Flourish', *BR*, Vol.27. No.50, 10 December, pp.18-21.

Ma Hung. (ed.). (1982), *A Dictionary of Economic Events in Modern China*, Beijing, China Social Sciences Press.

Ma Jisen. (1988), 'A General Survey of the Resurgence of Private Sector of China's Economy', *SSIC*, Autumn.

Mountjoy, Alan B. (1982), *Industrialization and Developing Countries*, Hutchinson, London.

Mo Tiansong. (1985), 'On the Tax Burden of the Rural and Small Town Enterprises', Beijing, *ZGSW*, No 5, 12 May, pp.31-32.

Mo Zhen. (1986), 'Tighten Control Over Big Labour-Hiring Households in Rural Areas', *KJGLYJ*, 10 February, pp.7-10, translated in *Chinese Economic Studies*, Winter 1987-88/Vol.XXI, No.2. pp.90-99.

Nan Bei. (1989), 'Capital Fundraising Conditions under a Tight Credit Regime', *JJRB*, 10 January.

Naya, Seiji. (1984), *Small-scale industries in Asian Economic Development: Problems and Prospects*, Economics Office Report Series, No. 24, Manila: Asian Development Bank.

Neck, Philip A (1977), *Small Enterprise Development: Policies and Programs*, International Labour Office, Geneva.

Nie Lisheng. (1988), 'State Acts to Regulate Private Businesses', *CD*, 26 May.

Niu Genying. (1991), 'Progress in China's Economic Reform', *BR*, 11-17 November, pp.11-14.

NMRB. (13 November 1986), 'Serious Problems of Small Retained Profits and Inadequate Reserve Strength in Enterprises -- Investigation on Profit Distribution in Town and Township Enterprises'.

NMRB. (22 December 1986), 'Several Suggestions on the Question of Township Enterprises' Profit Distributions'.

NMRB. (12 August 1987), 'Prejudice Against Town and Township Enterprises Should Be Removed'.

NMRB. (18 September 1987), 'Continue to Encourage the Development of Individually or Privately Owned Enterprises'.

NMRB. (15 December 1987), 'Serious Difficulties' in Development of Township Enterprises'.

Nolan, Peter and Dong Fureng. (eds). (1990), *Market Forces in China: Competition and Small Business -- The Wenzhou Debate*, Zed Books Ltd.

Ohkawa, Kazushi and Rosovsky, Henry. (1973), *Japanese Economic Growth*, Stanford University Press.

Pairault,Thieery. (1984), 'Chinese Market Mechanism: A Controversial Debate', in Maxwell, Neville & Mcfarlane, Bruce. (eds), *China's Changed Road to Development*, Pergamon Press, pp.35-41.

Parris, K. (1993), 'Local Initiative and National Reform: The Wenzhou Model of Development', *CQ*, June, pp. 242-263.

Prybyla, Jan S. (1989), 'China's Economic Experiment: Back from the Market?' *PC*, January-February, pp.1-18.

Qi Zong. (1982), 'Commune and Brigade Run Industry in China's Rural Areas', in Xue Muqiao. (ed.), *Almanac of China's Economy 1981 with Economic Statistics for 1949-1980*, Eurasia Press, pp.481-485.

Qiu Jian. (1988), 'The Rural Markets of Wenzhou', *CR*, November.

Qu Yingpu. (1988), 'Township Goods Must Make the Grade', *CD*, 15 March.

Rawski, Thomas G. (1979), *Economic Growth and Employment in China*, Oxford University Press.

Rawski, Thomas G. (1980), 'Choice of Technology and Technological Innovation in China's Economic Development', in Dernberger, Robert F. (ed), *China's Development Experience in Comparative Perspective*, Harvard University Press.

Riskin, Carl. (1971), 'Small Industry and the Chinese Model of Development', *CQ*, No.46, pp.245-273.

Riskin, Carl. (1978), 'China's Rural Industries: Self-reliant System or Independent Kingdoms', *CQ*, No.73, pp.77-98.

RMRB. (4 April 1978), 'It Is Necessary to Develop Greatly Enterprises Run by Commune and Production Brigades'.

RMRB. (27 September 1978), 'A Way to Develop Agriculture at High Speed'.

RMRB. (24 September 1979), 'Make Good Arrangements for Rural Autumn Markets'.

RMRB. (2 May 1981). 'A Strategic Measure for Invigorating the Rural Economy'.

RMRB. (10 April 1983), 'Several Problems in Current Rural Economic Policy (Central Document No. 1 for 1983)'.

RMRB. (19 May 1984), 'Actively Develop Enterprises in Town and Townships'.

RMRB. (27 October 1984), 'Attention Should Be Paid to the Big Market in the Countryside'.

RMRB. (6 December 1984), 'It Is good for Peasants to Go to Cities to Run Tertiary Industry'.

RMRB. (18 February 1985), 'Guard against Rushing Headlong into Mass Action'.

RMRB. (30 March 1985), 'Let Others Become Well-off Before Ourselves'.

RMRB. (20 April 1985), 'Provisional Income Tax Regulations Governing Collective Enterprises'.

RMRB. (24 September 1985), 'Chen Yuan's Speech'.

RMRB. (14 December 1985), 'Town and Township Enterprises Are not the 'Meat of the Buddhist Master of the Tang Dynasty'-Earnestly Solve the Problem of Heavy Burdens on Town and Township Enterprises'.

RMRB. (23 February 1986), 'The Plan of the CCP Central Committee and the State Council Concerning Rural work in 1986', (Overseas edition),.

RMRB. (5 June 1987), 'The Party's Rural Policies that Are in Force Are Correct and Stable'.

RMRB. (9 July 1987), 'Only When Some People Get Rich First Will There Be Common Prosperity'.

RMRB. (28 August 1987), 'Strengthen Order, Enliven the Market'.

RMRB. (19 August 1987), 'Safeguard and Promote the Healthy Development of the Individual Economy'.

RMRB. (23 August 87), 'Create More Employment Opportunities for Peasants'.

Rosen, Stanley. (1987), 'The Private Economy', *Chinese Economic Studies*, Fall, Vol. XXI, No.1.

Rweyemamu, J.F. (ed.). (1980), *Industrialization and Income Distribution in Africa*, Codesria, Dakar, Senegal.

Sandesara, J.C. (1988), 'Institutional Framework for Promoting Small-Scale Industries In India', *ADB*, Vol.6, No.2, pp.10-40.

Saich, Tony. (1989), *China's Science Policy in the 80s*, Humanities Press International, INC., 1989.

Shabad, Theodore. (1972), *China's Changing Map -- National and Regional Development, 1949-71*, Methuen & Co Ltd London.

Shi Ling. (1985), 'Xue Muqiao Puts Forward New Ideas on the Question of Ownership', *SJJJDB,* Shanghai, 9 December.

Shi Peihua. (1986), 'The Structure of Surplus Labour, and Counter-measures Against It', *JJWT*, No.12.

Sicular, Terry. (1985), 'Rural Marketing and Exchange in the Wake of Recent Reforms', in Elizabeth J.Perry and Christine Wong. (eds), *The Political Economy of Reform in Post-Mao China*, Harvard University Press, pp.83-109.

Sigurdson, Jon. (1977a), *Rural Industrialization in China*, Harvard University Press.

Sigurdson, Jon. (1977b), 'Transfer of Technology to the Rural and Collective Sectors in China', in *Science and Technology in the People's Republic of China*, OECD, pp.171-182.

Simon, Denis F. (1987), 'The Evolving Role of Reform in China's Science and Technology System', in Joseph. C.H. Chai and Chi-Keung Leung. (eds), *China's Economic Reform*, University of Hong Kong.

Song Lina and Du He. (1990), 'The Role of Township Governments in Rural Industrializations', in Byrd, William A. and Lin Qingsong. (eds), *China's Rural Industry -- Structure, Development, and Reform*, Oxford University Press, pp.342-357.

Staley, Eugene and Morse, Richard. (1965), *Modern Small Industry for Developing Countries*, International Student Edition, McGraw-hill, Tokyo.

Storey, D.J (1994), 'Public Policy', in Storey, D.J, Understanding the Small Business Sector, Routledge, London, pp.253-306.

Su Bei. (1989), 'The Township Enterprises, Where Are They Heading For?' *BYT*, No.19, pp.32-34.

Suhartono, R.B. (1988), 'Small and Medium-scale Industries in Indonesia', *ADB*, Vol. 6, No.2, pp.41-69.

Sun Jian. (1991), 'He Kang Answers Chinese, Foreign Reporters' Questions on Development of Township Enterprises', *ZGXZQYB*, 5 April.

Sun Xuewen. (1985), 'Establish a Co-ordinated and Flexible Economic Regulatory System', *GMRB*, 12 October.

Svejnar, Jan, and Woo, Josephine. (1990), 'Development Patterns in Four Counties', in William A. Byrd and Lin Qingsong. (eds), *China's Rural Industry -- Structure, Development, and Reform*, Oxford University Press, pp.63-84.

Tang Tsou, Blecher, Marc and Meisner, Mitch. (1982), 'National Agricultural Policy: The Dazhai Model and Local Change in the Post-Mao Era', in Mark Selden and Victor Lippit, *The Transition to Socialism in China*, M.E.Sharpe, Inc., Armonk, New York.

Taylor, Jeffrey R. (1988), 'Rural Employment Trends and the Legacy of Surplus Labour, 1978-86', *CQ*, No.116, December, pp.736-766.

TE. (10 December 1988), 'Winning in Wenzhou', Vol.309, No.7580, pp.70-73.

TE. (11 February 1989), 'Privatising China', Vol.310, No.7589, p.70.

TE. (1 June 1991), 'China's Economy: They Couldn't Keep It Down', Vol.319, No.7709, pp.17-20.

TE. (22 June 1991), 'Sons of the Soil', Vol.319, No.7712, p.68.

The Minister of Agriculture, Animal Husbandry and Fishery and the Ministry's Leading Party Group. (1984), 'Report on Creating a New Situation for Commune and Brigade enterprises', *SWB/FE*, 26 March.

The State Council. (1984), 'Certain Regulations Governing Individual Industry and Commerce in Rural Areas', *SWB/FE*, 19 March.

The State Statistical Bureau, PRC, (1985), *Statistical Yearbook of China 1985*, Oxford University Press.

The State Statistical Bureau. (1988), *Statistical Yearbook of China 1988* (Chinese Edition), Chinese Statistical Press.

The World Bank, *China--Between Plan and Market*, 1990.

Tu Xinjun. (1987), 'The Rise of Township Industries and the New Issues They Face', *SJJJDB*, 18 May.

Tung, Ricky (1994), 'The Development of Rural Shareholding Cooperative Enterprises in Mainland', *IS*, Vol.30, No.5, pp.1-30.

Ullerich, Curtis. (1979), *Rural Employment and Manpower Problems in China*, M.E.Sharpe inc Dawson.

United Nations Industrial Development Organization (UNIDO). (1969), *Small Scale Industry*, UNIDO Monographs on Industrial Development, No.11, New York: United Nations.

Wang Dacheng. (1985), 'Chinese Peasants Favour Small Towns', *BR*, No.13, 1 April.

Wang Dongtai. (1992), 'Rural Industries Boost Production by 36%', *CD*, 21 April.

Wang Huning, (1988a), 'An Economic Analysis of the Reform of China's Political-Administrative System', *SHKXZX*, No. 2, pp.107-115.

Wang Huning, (1988b), 'Ramifications of Changing Relationship Between Central and Local Government in China', *Fudan Xuebao*(Fudan University Journal), No.5, pp.1-8, p.30.

Wang Jian. (1990), 'Assessment of the Development of China's Township Enterprises in 1990', *LW*, Overseas Edition, No.49, 3 December, pp.3-4.

Wang Shuwei. (1986), 'A Summary of the Discussion on the Labour Force Market', *GMRB*, 2 August.

Wang Tuoyu. (1990), 'Regional Imbalances', in William A.Byrd and Lin Qingsong. (eds), *China's Rural Industry -- Structure, Development, and Reform*, Oxford University Press, pp.255-273.

Wang Youfen and Li Ning. (1986), 'Bottons Work Miracles in Wenzhou', *BR*, No.42, 20 October.

Wang Zhonghui. (1990), 'Private Enterprise in China: An Overview', *JCS*, Vol.6, No.3, pp.83-98.

Wang Zhonghui. (1993), 'China's Policies Towards Collective Rural Enterprises', *SED*, Vol.4, No.1, pp. 16-26.

Wang Zhonghui. (1995), 'Township Public Finance and Its Impact on the Financial Burden of Rural Enterprises and Peasants in Mainland China', *IS*, Vol.31, No.8, pp.103-121.

Wen Jia. (1989), 'Private Business Suffers Setback', *CD*, 29 April.

Wen Quan. (1986), 'Tentative Views on 'Centralization' in the Rural Economy', *GMRB*, 7 September.

Wen Tianshen. (1992), 'China's 'Second Revolution' ', *CT*, February, pp.14-17.

Wu Jinglian and Zhao Renwei. (1988), 'The Dual Pricing System in China's Industry', in Bruce L.Reynolds. (ed.), *Chinese Economic Reform -- How Far, How Fast?* Academic Press, INC., pp.19-28.

Wu Mingyu. (1986), 'A Fundamental Policy for Promoting the Technological Progress of Township Enterprises--a Few Points of Understanding on the Spark Plan', *RMRB*, 27 January.

Wu Peilun. (1986), 'The Experience of Developing Small and Medium-sized Cities in My County', *RMRB*, Overseas Edition, 14 June.

Wu Quhui, Wang Hansheng and Xu Xinxin. (1990), 'Noneconomic Determinants of Workers' Incomes', in William A.Byrd and Lin Qingsong. (eds), *China's Rural Industry -- Structure, Development, and Reform*, Oxford University Press, pp.323-337.

Wu Xiang. (1986), 'On the Developing Rural Commodity Economy in Wenzhou', *RMRB*, 4 August.

Wu Yunhe. (1989a), 'Profits Leak Out of Rural Pockets', *CD*, 23 January.

Wu Yunhe. (1989b), 'Townships Told to Develop Exports', *CD*, 25 September.

XHYB. (1988), 'Provisional Regulations on Private Enterprises of The People's Republic of China', No.6.

XHYB. (1990), 'Regulations on Township and Village Collective Ownership Enterprises in the PRC', No.6.

Xio Li. (1986), 'China's Approach to Solving the Employment Pressure in the Countryside', Hongkong, *LW*, Overseas Edition, 28 July.

Xiao Lan. (1986), 'Hope and Fears of Township and Town Industries in the Course of Technological Progress', *JJGZTX*, No.21, 15 November, pp.23-24.

Xiao Liang. (1985), 'Superficial Views on Ownership of Economic Combinations', *GMRB*, 9 November.

Xu Hongsheng. (1984), 'An Analysis of Fixing Production According to Marketing', *RMRB*, 28 May.

Xu Muqiao. (1985), 'A Talk with Consumers on the Question of Commodity Prices', *RMRB*, 10 October.

Xu Shanda. (1987), 'Tax Policies Related to the Township Enterprises and Their Tax Burdens', *NYJJWT*, No.9.

Xu Yu. (1987), 'Township Enterprises and Foreign Trade', *GJMYWT*, No 6, pp. 16-20.

Xue Muqiao. (1987), 'Socialism and Planned Commodity Economy', *BR*, Vol.30, No.39, 28 September.

Yang Dali. (1990), 'Patterns of China's Regional Development Strategy', *CQ*, No. 122, June, pp.230-257.

Yang Yi. (1988), 'Private Banks Cash in on Trial Policy in Wenzhou', *CD*, 29 November.

Yan Nong. (1983), 'The Development of the 'Two Households and One Alliance' in Rural Hebei', *SHKXDT*, June, p.13.

Yan Yingeong. (1987), 'Coordinated Development of Urban and Rural Enterprises in South Jiangsu', *NYJJWT*, No.11.

Yeh Kung-Chia (1990), 'Capital Shortage in Mainland China: Nature, Causes, and Prospects', in King-yuh Chang (ed.), *Mainland China After the Thirteenth Party Congress*, Westview Press, pp.359-377.

You Ji. (1991), 'Zhao Ziyang and the Politics of Inflation', *AJCA*, No.25, January, pp.69-91.

Young, Susan. (1989), 'Policy, Practice and The Private Sector in China', *AJCA*, No.21, January, pp.57-80.

Yu Guangyuan. (1986), 'Put Price Ahead of Value', *JJYJ*, 20 May.

Yu Guoyao and Li Yandong. (1989), 'The Difficulties and Problems Facing Township and Town Enterprises', *NYJJWT*, No.10, 23 October, pp.22-27.

Yun Yeo-Gyeong. (1988), 'Promoting Small and Medium Industries: The Korean Experience', *ADB*, Vol.6, No.2, pp.96-109.

ZGXZQYB. (15 January 1986), 'Shift Focus of Work to Product Quality; Report on Product Quality Inspection in Jiangsu and Shandong Township and Town Enterprises'.

ZGXZQYB. (12 March 1986), 'Opinions on Strengthening Product Quality Management Work in Township and Town Industries'.

Zhan Wu and Liu Wenpu. (1984), 'Agriculture -- Chinese Agriculture Before 1976', in Yu Guangyuan. (eds), *China's Socialist Modernization*, Foreign Languages Press, Beijing.

Zhai Feng. (1992), 'New Blueprint for Rural Firms', *CD*, 9 April.

Zhang Jihai. (1987), 'Distribution of Township Enterprises is a Problem Deserving Greater Attention', *JJCK*, 20 October.

Zhang Pengfa. (1986), 'Changes In Private Enterprises Underline the Need to Tighten Control of Industry and Commerce in Rural Areas', *GSXZGL*, 1 September 1986, translated in *CES*, Winter 1987-88/Vol.XXI, No.2, pp.62-64.

Zhang Xiaogang. (1987), 'Moves Seek to Promote Farm Area Industries', *CD*, 9 November.

Zhang Xiaoli and Liu Yaguang. (1986), 'Industrial Subsidy of Agriculture is the Strategic Measure to Stabilize Agriculture', *SCRB*, 15 September.

Zhang Zeyu. (1987), 'The Role of Private Enterprises', *BR*, Vol.30, No.39.

Zhang Kewen. (1988), 'Private Enterprise in the Spotlight', *CD*, 27 May.

Zhao Ziyang. (1987), 'Advance Along the Road of Socialism with Chinese Characteristics - Report Delivered at the Thirteenth National Congress of the Communist Party of China Concerning the Report of the Twelfth Central Committee of China on 25 October 1987', *in Documents of the Thirteenth National Congress of the Communist Party of China (25 October - 1 November 1987)*, Foreign Languages Press, Beijing.

Zheng Pujing. (1989), 'To Develop Rural Enterprises Through the Progress of Technology & Science', *ZGJJWT*, No.5.

Zhou Qiren and Hu Zhuangjun. (1989), 'Asset Formation and Operational Features of Industrial Enterprises in Chinese Townships and Their Macro-effects', *SSIC*, No.2, p.116.

Zhu Qingfang. (1986), 'On the Evolution and Changes of Individual Economy and Countermeasures', *JJYJCKZL*, No.66, pp.33-40.

Zweig, David. (1991), 'Internationalizing China's Countryside: The Political Economy of Exports From Rural Industry', *CQ*, No.126, June, pp.716-741.

Index

NB: No entries are given for the following: 'agricultural/agriculture', 'labour', 'policy/policies', 'rural enterprises', since their page references are too numerous to include in the Index.

150